# How to bunny proof your home

# Living with a house bunny

## Indoor enclosures

## Toys and games

Thank you for buying our book. We are a husband and wife team that have been keeping house rabbits for over 20 years. We hope to share this experience and the lessons we have learnt along the way ourselves and with our friends in our Facebook group, which at this time has over 9,000 members.

Special thanks to Amanda Waters for her support in the creation of this book. We dedicate this book to our bunnies that have offered us companionship and showed us how to live better lives together. We would also like to thank all the bunnies and their owners in our facebook group who have contributed.

# How to stop your bunny chewing electrical cables

## Inside this article

It is important for your bunnies health and happiness that you share lots of time together, for most people this involves relaxing at home in front of the TV or listening to music with your bunny roaming in the room.

Unfortunately, the cables that power these electrical devices can be very harmful, even deadly if your bunny chews on them, unaware of the danger.

The soft plastic insulation offers no protection from a bunnies razor sharp teeth that are perfect for slicing through tough roots and shoots and if their wet mouth comes into contact with the wires inside they can receive a severe shock.

**Obi and Alisa**
My buns (mostly one in particular) are super chewers.

The only safe way to share your home with your bunny is to fully bunny proof it and, in this guide, we show you how.

We have some great tips on how to hide power cables out of reach by simply moving some of your furniture around or by breaking up some pet pen fencing.

We have details on using box conduite and split length pipe to protect exposed cables.

We even show you how to block off the crawl spaces around the back of your TV which can be especially dangerous for a curious bunny.

So, don't take the chance of an accident happening, get bunny proofing so you can relax with your bunny roaming freely without having to unplug everything first.

## Keep cables out of reach behind your furniture

The easiest way to stop your bunny chewing the electrical cables in your home is to make some simple changes to the way your furniture is laid out to make them inaccessible.

By arranging furniture and electrical devices together you can limit the amount of exposed cables your bunny can reach.

Move furniture with lamps or other electrical devices directly in front of plug sockets so you can lead the electrical cables from the plug to conceal them.

Make sure you push the furniture up against the wall as bunnies like to explore these gaps.

You can also trail cables over or behind furniture by moving it closer together to help keep them out of reach.

When you are done make sure you move everything out the way that could provide an alternative route for your bunny to get to exposed cables.

Bunnies are good climbers and can jump from place to place so always do a quick check to be safe.

Lastly, always remember to find a safe place to put your bunny when ironing, hovering, or using a hair dryer or other appliances.

It only takes a moment's distraction for the damage to be done.

## How to stop your bunny going behind your TV

Bunnies love to explore and no amount of saying No! will keep them out of forbidden areas like behind your TV when your back is turned.

It's best to always block this area off entirely so the nest of electrical cables they contain are permanently out of harm's reach.

### Hugo
We were wondering why our internet was buggy.

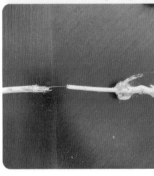 

Position the TV against a wall in front of a plug or in the corner where a plug socket is so you don't need to trail any cables up to it.

You can block off the sides of your TV to stop access behind with other bits of furniture or large ornaments. Alternatively you can use a couple of sections of a pet pen or the wire grids from office storage cubes either side.

It can help to keep all your TV and audio equipment together in a cabinet. Cabinets with glass doors are ideal as this will let you keep the doors shut and still use your remote controls.

Avoid blocking in the sides with cardboard as this will not last very long and may even encourage your bunny to play in this area.

If your bunny makes it a mission to try and go behind the TV you can help refocus this natural need to explore by providing some safe and acceptable alternatives such as tunnel toys, tents or even a cardboard castle to help keep them out of trouble.

## Keep electricals out of reach behind a simple pet pen fence

### Harvey
We have a section of our living room blocked off with a pen. Even though the pen is super low because the area behind it is so small, he doesn't jump over, even for his hay and pellets which we store behind there.

Fully bunny proofing all the electrical devices and electrical cables in a room can be a massive task to undertake.

Sometimes this can make it hard for you to access and use these devices yourself. A better way to manage areas with lots of electrical devices in it is to simply fence them off.

To do this take a regular pet pen and simply join the sections of sheets together as fencing using the clips provided.

If you set it out in a zigzag pattern this can even be free standing or lash the ends to some furniture using some cotton string.

### Rex
Your move, Rex! My husband made a lucite cover for the electronics and we used a very heavy cardboard tube for the cords.

If you have a computer desk or stacks of stereo equipment, create a fence that will screen off the whole area. Making sure the ends are secure so your bunny cannot force its way around.

Fencing can also be used to block access to crawl spaces that lead to plugs under furniture or behind an appliance. You can build a low fence using sections of wire grids. These can be lashed in place with some string.

Installing a baby gate across a door to an area with lots of electrical equipment such as a utility room can be a great way of blocking off access and still allowing you to nip in and out whilst keeping an eye on your bunny.

Avoid using cardboard as fencing as bunnies like to eat this and will eventually break through.

## The split length tubing hack

Protect electrical cables by slipping them inside some split length tubing.

Sometimes it is hard to avoid wires that stretch across your room or to your appliances on a shelf or furniture top.

A simple, convenient, and cheap way of adding protection is to slip your electrical cables inside a length of tough plastic piping or split length tubing as it is often called.

This piping can be purchased from most DIY stores. It is tough and just flexible enough to be bent around corners.

You can often find brands of pipe that have already been split along its length, if not you will need to cut it yourself.

To install it first cut the tubing to the correct length then you can simply slip the wire inside along the split without having to take the plug off.

You can make it safer by securing the ends with some tape in case your bunny tugs at it leaving the electrical cables by the plug exposed.

**Chester The Dexter**
Chester The Dexter at the hardware store. Tubing in the cart

## Box conduit, a neat way to make cables safe

Plastic conduit is an ideal solution if you want to add some permanent bunny proof to your home.

The tough strips of boxing or piping can be mounted on a wall above your baseboards and electrical cables that would otherwise lead around the edges of the room can be hidden away inside, keeping them safe.

Make sure you not only fit them around the room but also leading down from plug sockets then up the wall behind furniture where electrical devices are so once the electrical cables inside are safely out of reach.

They are relatively cheap and can be purchased from most DIY stores and can be installed with a minimum of effort.

**Ernie**
I use cable channels and flex tubing, as well as baby-proofing outlet covers. As a warning, my rabbit had chewed through flex tubing a couple times, so check it periodically for chew marks.

The soft plastic can be easily trimmed to size and these systems typically come with a variety of corners and junctions that make it easy to assemble.

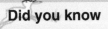

### Did you know

### Why does my bunny chew my electrical cables?

Rabbits have razor sharp teeth that they use to chew through tough roots and shoots. They do this for food and to keep their burrows and paths clear of obstacles to help them move about.

Unfortunately for your bunny, electrical cables are pretty much the same size as a root and shoot and they often lay in your bunnies path at the edges of the room where they run into them. This makes them almost irritable to rabbits and the moment they come across one their natural urge to chew through it is likely to take over.

## How to bunny proof your phone charger

There is no good way of protecting the cables that charge or power our gadgets from a bunny on the lookout for something to chew. The only way to keep them safe is to keep one step ahead and move them out of harm's reach.

Following these simple rules which in hindsight will prove expensive mistakes.

If you leave a charger in reach it is an accident waiting to happen. It is best to set yourself up a charging station somewhere completely out of reach like a kitchen worktop or a study room where your bunny does not have access and make this its permanent home.

### Rex

Rex killed Alexa. He doesn't look too guilty. I fished him out from behind the couches with a treat... it was too easy. Now, did I feed him the treat or not? I can't remember.

We tend to give our phones and other devices a lot of attention so always remember to put them out of reach when you are done. Bunnies are very curious, and by curious I mean have a quick chew on anything at least once.

Lastly, never rely on telling your bunny off or using bitter sprays to stop your bunny chewing electrical cables. It wont stop them. Only hiding away the cables will make it totally safe.

### Milo
Spicy hay!

### Bunny proof checklist
- [x] Hide plug sockets behind furniture then trail power cable out of reach.
- [x] Remember bunnies are good climbers and can jump quite high.
- [x] It can be easier to fence off whole areas of a room with sections of pet pen.
- [x] Always block off access behind your TV.
- [x] You can protect exposed cords with Split length tubing or Box conduit.

# How to stop your bunny chewing your carpet

## Inside this article

Carpet chewing is a very common problem for people with house bunnies and sometimes it can be quite a battle to keep them looking neat.

In this guide we show you the various ways other bunny parents use to stop their bunnies from what can seem an unstoppable desire to dig and chew their carpet and prevent the substantial damage this can cause over time.

We have some simple solutions like, using an old ceramic tile to cover over a trouble spot.

We also have a guide to the Pros and Cons of floor covering that are commonly used to cover carpet to protect them completely from chewing and stains.

**Cocoa**
Mine likes to chill by the beach, sometimes he guards the supermarket...

If you think using a taste deterrent like a bitter spray could help, we also show you what to use and the best way to apply it.

So if you do have a bunny that's a bit of a carpet chewer or just want to make sure you don't lose your deposit, here's how to put a stop to carpet chewing with some effective bunny proofing.

## Protecting areas where your bunny chews your carpet

If there is an area of carpet your bunny seems to keep picking on, then a lot of people have found a simple way to stop the damage continuing any further this to laying a spare ceramic over the spot.

Quick and easy carpet protection

The weight of the tile will also help stop the carpet being tugged up which can cause a lot of damage if your bunny gets their teeth into it. Tiles are good as they are cheap, don't get in the way and can be easily packed away when not needed.

Another easy way to stop your bunny chewing carpet can simply be to place a cardboard box over the top. This will effectively stop your bunny getting to the carpet and hopefully give it something more fun to do that is an acceptable alternative to both of you.

## The best ways of covering your carpet to stop damage

If you want to be sure to stop your bunny chewing your carpet you are best to cover it over completely.

This can be especially useful if you have a room or night-time pen where your bunny spends a lot of time unsupervised.

Carpet end rolls make an ideal covering

There are a number of ways that bunny owners have found to do this.

An obvious way to cover your carpet and protect it is to lay down some rugs or mats. Choose a rug made from a natural material such as wool or cotton in case it gets chewed as synthetic material can cause digestive problems if eaten.

It is often best to weigh down the corners to stop the rug being pulled up and the carpet uncovered.

Some bunny owners who want something to totally protect their carpet from chewing and damage from spillages and peeing accidents have found that children's play mats make an attractive, waterproof covering that can be wiped clean.

I buy the black plastic sheets from Home Depot. Tape down to protect carpet/hardwood floor from accidents. Then buy inexpensive carpet remnants to put on top. The remnants are cheap and easy to switch out as needed. I also put padding in since it is a hard wood floor and I want the buns to have cushions. I did actually wrap the padding in plastic too, cause momma bunny tends to pee in the corners.....That way I don't have to replace the padding too, only the carpet itself.

If you want to cover a larger area and want to keep the cost low, you could always see if your local carpet store has any cheap roll ends.

## Lucky

Just be careful with vinyl flooring. One of our bunnies that was adopted out of our rescue recently had to go to the vet with stasis. The x-ray showed he had bits of vinyl flooring and towel he had ingested after chewing. My buns are in my family room. There's old very low pile carpet in there and they don't chew it. Probably because it's so ugly! LOL! But I'm not changing it.

Other alternatives people have found that may work for you are horse mats that are very tough and outdoor carpet that you can buy from home improvement stores.

## What to use to protect your carpet from bunny chewing

- Rugs and throws, and fleece blankets
- Children's play mats
- Horse mats
- Carpet roll ends
- Outdoor carpet
- Puzzle mats, used for child play areas

## Also see

**65** What is the best floor for my bunny enclosure?

## Using bitter sprays to help stop chewing

Bitter sprays can be used to make chewing your carpet a little less appealing.

Unfortunately, in most cases people find that it is not a single solution and works best alongside some of the other bunny proofing.

It's best to apply the spray directly to the areas where the damage is being caused and any other areas that look like likely targets.

Remember to keep reapplying it as it will lose its effectiveness.

**Mr Cuddles**
It went from this to destroyed every single edge of my daughters room

Avoid home-made taste deterrents that may be suggested to you such as perfume or chilly oil or soap as these can be harmful to your bunny, instead choose a recognized brand designed for bunnies.

### How do I tell my bunny off for eating carpet

- Only tell your bunny off when you catch them chewing your carpet.
- Be careful not to scare your bunny when telling them off, stress can make them timid or aggressive towards you.
- Never hit or push your bunny away forcefully from the patch of carpet they are chewing, bunnies are very delicate and can be hurt easily.
- Why not build a digging box for your bunny to exercise their natural digging and foraging behavior.

**Lil Z**
3 course meal done Nice bit of floor mat for starters, hay ball for the main, then a nice helping of nuggets for dessert and his so stuffed he's collapsed

Is your bunny building a nest? Some bunnies especially Does like to pull up soft materials like carpet strands as a part of their instinctive nesting behavior when they are pregnant or having a phantom pregnancy. Give your bunny a stack of hay or an old towel to use as an acceptable alternative to keep them out of trouble.

**Did you know**

**What should I do if my bunny starts eating my carpet**

If you discover your carpet is on the menu for your bunny you will need to cover it with something your bunny will leave alone or restrict access to this area.

Unfortunately many of the synthetic material carpet is made of can cause digestive problems if eaten by your bunny. Long strands of indigestible string and foam backing can all cause you bunny to be unwell.

**Bunny proof checklist**
- [x] Cover areas of damaged carpet with a spare ceramic tile or cardboard box to protect it.
- [x] Use rugs, carpet roll-ends or play mats to permanently protect areas of carpet from damage.
- [x] Bitter sprays can help make areas of carpet that are being chewed less appealing.

# Help! How do I repair my carpet where my bunny has chewed it?

**Inside this article**

It's surprising how quickly chewing damage can spread if your bunny takes a liking to a spot of carpet to chew, especially if it happens unnoticed behind a sofa or under a bed. Don't panic there are ways to fix this and with a bit of know-how you can restore the damage at no cost.

Follow these guides and see how you can easily repair small patches of nibbled carpet.

Or see how to swap out a section of carpet if the problem is bigger with a spare bit in a cupboard.

We have details on the tools and other stuff you need so you can do a proper repair job and restore the damage as good as new.

**Snowy**
Guilty

## Repair small patches of carpet

If it's a small patch of carpet, an inch or so across, a simple way to fix this is to take a pair of scissors and from around your carpet carefully cut out the odd strand at the base. Make sure you spread this out so it will go unnoticed. Next using some strong glue start to build the carpet back up by gluing the strands back in one at the base. With a bit of patience, you will soon build the pile up again.

## How to repair large patches of carpet

If it's a larger patch it can be best to replace the section with new carpet. Ideally you may have some spare carpet but if not, you may find that the same carpet has been used in a cupboard or under a piece of furniture and you can use this instead.

To make sure it fits perfectly take the replacement piece and check to see if there is a noticeable grain as you will need to line this up with the grain of the carpet.

Cut around the area you want to replace using a utility knife. Cutting through carpet can be tricky so you may need to score it a few times. If you can lift the edges up as you cut this will help avoid cutting into the carpet padding beneath. It's best to cut out an odd shape like a triangle as square shaped replacements tend to be more noticeable.

Cut a new piece of carpet the same shape. It can be helpful to make it slightly larger than the hole, if you have a limited amount of carpet you can always trim it down a bit however a piece smaller than the hole will be noticeable.

Make sure any missing underlay has been glued back in first then apply adhesive to the back of the carpet and to the carpet edges that surround the hole you cut out.

Orientate the new piece of carpet so the grain runs in the same direction as the installed carpet, then press the patch firmly down.

When it is dry you can ruffle the edges up a bit, so it blends in.

# How to stop your bunny chewing your baseboards

**Inside this article**

The soft wooden edges of your baseboards can be irresistible to a bored bunny and it only takes a few nibbles for noticeable damage to be done. Over time a bunny on a mission can do a lot of damage.

Bunnies spend a lot of time foraging around the edge of a room so it can be impossible to guard them all the time which is why bunny proofing is the only way to keep them safe and your home looking neat.

In this guide we show you some quick and easy ways to protect troubled spots like using a ceramic tile to cover an area until you can refocus attention on a more suitable alternative.

Get bunny proofing before your baseboards end up on the menu

We also show you how to add permanent types of protection such as plastic corner guards and how to stop wooden steps getting chewed and how bitter spray can be used to help tackle this problem.

If you bunny is a bit of a chewer then here is everything you need to know to stop the chewing damage.

## How to use a ceramic tile to quickly stop the chewing

Problems spots where your bunny has chewed your baseboards can pop up anywhere especially around door frames or areas where you bunny sits.

As soon as you notice a spot developing its best to try and stop it quickly before it develops.

Repurposed bunny toys used to stop chewing

An easy way to add some temporary protection is to prop up a few ceramic tiles against the areas your bunny has taken an interest in.

They are heavy enough to stay in place and can be easily packed away when not needed.

Willow bridges, a cheap toy found in pet stores can be another useful way of protecting baseboards.

They can even be bent into an L shape to follow the edge of a baseboard around a corner.

A cardboard box can be another great way to protect a trouble spot. Simply place it over the area being damaged.

Make sure you weigh down the box by placing something heavy inside.

Bunnies can be surprisingly strong when they want to get to something they want to chew.

## Permanent ways of protecting your baseboards

### Bunny mom

Just wanted to share this baseboard hack with you all! Maybe this will help some of you! I bought these plastic baseboards at Home Depot for about $3-4 a 6ft piece, stuck some Velcro and voila. Easy to clean, easy on the eye and best of all BUN PROOF (even for my smartest bun) he will chew on them a bit but I don't think it's as satisfying of a crunch as baseboards so he leaves them be for the most part. Bun mom 1, Bun 32.

If you want to make sure your baseboards will not be chewed it's best to try and protect them permanently with something chew proof.

An ideal way to do this is to install some corner guards. These strips of L shaped plastic can be found in most home stores and can be easily cut to length using a craft knife and attached with some sticky pads. They come in a wood color, white and clear so you will be able to match it with your baseboards.

Another way people go about stopping their baseboard being chewed is to build a small fence around the outside of the room with some sections of office storage cubes.

### Ozric

Some bunnies won't take NO! for an answer

These foot square grids come in packs of 12 and can be easily tied together in a long series with the small cable ties that get supplied with them.

This fence can then be set out a short distance from the edge of the room leaving just enough gap to make the baseboards unreachable.

## How to apply bitter sprays

Bitter sprays can be helpful if you are battling to stop your bunny chewing your baseboards but don't expect this to stop the problem in itself as you may find your bunny more than prepared to put up with a bad taste.

### What is the best things to use to protect your baseboards from bunny chewing

- Plastic corner guards
- Decorative baseboard covers
- A ceramic tile rested up against it
- Cardboard box
- Repurposed Willow bridge bunny toy
- Wire grids or pet pen fence
- Bitter spray

### Peter and Parsnip

How do I get them to stop this? My bonded pair free roam (and have for months) but lately have been interior decorating and chewing up the walls.

## How do I tell my bunny off for chewing my baseboards

- Only tell your bunny No! when you catch them in the act or they may not know why you are telling them off.
- Never scare or shock your bunny to try and stop them chewing your baseboards, stress can make them unfriendly towards you.
- Never hit your bunny or push them away, they don't respond well to physical punishment and you could hurt them very easily.

Avoid homemade remedies that may be suggested to you such as perfume or chilly oil or soap as these can be harmful to your bunny and instead use a product designed for bunnies.

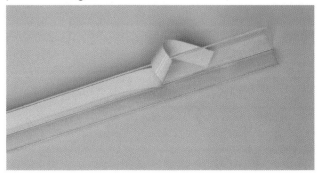

Add a bit of protection with some corner guards

## Also see

**40** Using bitter spray to stop your bunny chewing carpet, wallpaper, baseboards and furniture

**51** How to use a water mister to train and discipline your bunny

## How to protect wooden steps and banisters

**George and Jeremy**
Aluminum angle strip from Bunnings. My new best friend

Damage from your bunny chewing your wooden steps or the edges of your wooden banisters can also be a common problem for free roaming house bunnies.

Fortunately, there are lots of home improvement solutions that can be repurposed as bunny proofing that are designed to stop wear and tear.

Most home stores stock a range of corner protectors for steps that are cheap and can be fitted without needing extensive DIY skills or tools.

These range from anti slip mats that lip over the edge to aluminum edging that can be fitted as a permanent solution.

Banister rails can be fenced off with sections of wire grids or sections of pet pen fencing.

### Did you know

### Why does my bunny eat my baseboards

Rabbits love to chew on soft wood as it helps wear down and sharpen their teeth, which constantly grow throughout their lives. They also chew soft wooden materials as a source of dietary fiber which makes up most of their diet.

Baseboards are not only made of soft wood with easy to nibble corners they also lie at just the right height for your rabbit to stubble into so unfortunately, they often end up on the menu.

### Bunny proof checklist
- [x] Rest a ceramic tile over a trouble spot to quickly protect it.
- [x] Protect soft wooden edges from being chewed by installing some tough plastic corner guards.
- [x] Wooden steps can be protected with anti-slip mats or edging strips.
- [x] Applying bitter sprays can make the taste a lot less appealing.

# How to stop your bunny chewing walls and wallpaper

**Inside this article**

Bunnies, especially bored ones are always on the lookout for something fibrous to chew, it helps wear down her teeth and supplements their diet with fiber which they need to keep healthy.

Unfortunately, in your bunnies eyes wallpaper and even your walls look ideal for this and if they learn to strip off the paper and scrape away the plaster then in no time at all you can be looking at a significant amount of damage.

These natural urges if they start can be hard to stop no matter how many times you tell your bunny to stop. This is why the only real option is to bunny proof areas of your walls to stop your bunny chewing them.

**Dobby**
Some bunny is in BIG, BIG trouble today!!

In this guide we show you the many ways other bunny parents have gone about protecting their wallpaper.

We have some simple ideas like fence a wall off with some sections of pet pen or wire grids.

We also have a guide on how to fix more permanent protection such as fitting corner guards as well as examples of using clear acrylic.

We also show you the best ways to use bitter sprays and have a guide to the best test determinants.

Follow the guide here to learn how you can keep your wallpaper intact and be able to spend time with your bunny without the worry.

## Simple ideas to stop your bunny chewing your wallpaper

A cardboard box is probably the simplest way to block access to an area of a wall.

It's best to put something heavy in it to stop it being moved around as bunnies can be surprisingly strong when something is in their way.

A simple way to provide temporary protection is to keep a few ceramic tiles handy and lay them up against the walls in these areas.

These can then be packed away when not needed.

Section of office cube storage or pet pen can be used to fence off an area

Or another great way to cover over an area that won't look as out of place is to use a common toy often called a willow bridge to lean up against the wall.

These toys made of a series of willow sticks linked together are heavy enough to not be moved about by a bunny

They will give them a tasty alternative to chew on that's hopefully tastier than another part of the wall that's unprotected.

A very common way to protect large areas of walls and wallpaper in your home is simply to fence them off with sections of pet pen.

You can break out sections of a pen to get the right sized fence.

If you want something a bit shorter you can also use sections of office storage cubes.

### Did you know

### Why does my bunny chew my wallpaper

It is important for a rabbit's health to eat a wide range of fibrous materials. This is not only good for their digestion but also helps wear down their teeth which can grow up to 5 inches a year.

Wallpaper unfortunately is something you bunny may choose to eat as a part of its diet. Always provide lots of alternative chew toys and a stack of hay each day.

## Permanently ways to stop protect against chewing

A permanent and neat looking solution to protecting your walls and wallpaper from your bunnies unwanted chewing and scratching is to mount some sheets of clear acrylic to them.

This can work well if you have built a large pen that uses a wall as a part of its perimeter.

If you have some DIY skills, clear plastic sheeting makes a great permanent solution to wallpaper chewing

This will require some DIY skills but will protect your walls from chewing, scratching and general mess that may spread about.

### Using bitter sprays to stop wall chewing

**Misty**
If you can't beat em then join em. I stripped the walls and painted them

Bitter sprays can help make walls and wallpaper a lot less appealing for a bored bunny to chew on however, it is not likely to stop chewing damage completely on its own so should be used alongside other remedies.

Apply the treatment to areas that are being chewed and anywhere else you think could become a target. Remember to re apply it frequently to stop it wearing off.

Avoid homemade remedies such as perfume or chilly oil and instead use a recognized bitter spray which is designed for bunnies and remember to keep reapplying the bitter spray regularly so it doesn't lose its effectiveness.

## Demolition girl

Woke up to bunny demolition this am. How in the hell did she reach it?! Now I have to stress over obstruction?! Most pieces seem accounted for. Does she not look so innocent?

## Also see

**40** Using bitter spray to stop your bunny chewing carpet, wallpaper, baseboards and furniture

## How to tell your bunny off for chewing your walls and wallpaper

- Only tell your bunny off when you catch them chewing your wallpaper or they will not understand.
- Never scare or cause your bunny stress as this may make them timid or aggressive towards you.
- Even if you bunny is being naughty never hit or push or chase your bunny away, they spook easily and can hurt themselves in the rush to get away.
- Why not build a digging box with lots of things to shred and chew in.

## How to stop corner chewing

If your bunny has started to nibble at the paper on the corner of your walls it is best to act quickly to stop this before it spreads across the wall or the plaster gets eaten. To do this it's best to protect your walls with something chew resistant.

Fortunately, a simple way to protect fragile edges is to use a cheap commercial product designed specifically to stop this type of damage.

You may have seen these L shaped lengths of tough plastic in public buildings and you can buy them in most DIY stores and fit them yourself.

Never underestimate how much damage your bunny can do when they start a project

They come in a variety of lengths however you only need to cover up to your bunnies reach so it's best to cut down to size. This can be done with a craft knife so no need for any DIY tools.

They can then be easily attached to the wall with some sticky pads or adhesive.

They also come in a variety of colors so you can match your wall or in clear so they can go over patterned wallpaper without standing out.

These tough plastic corner guards from DIY stores are ideal for protect the corners from chewing

## Bunny proof checklist

- ☒ Temporarily protect wallpaper by placing a ceramic tile or cardboard box in the way.
- ☒ Build a fence around the edge of your room with some sections of pet pen or office storage cubes
- ☒ If you want to permanently protect your walls you may consider mounting acrylic sheeting.
- ☒ Protect exposed corners with plastic corner guards.
- ☒ Apply some bitter spray to areas being chewed to act as a deterrent.

# How to stop your bunny chewing and damaging your couch

**Inside this article**

It can be very hard to stop your bunny chewing and trying to burrow into your couch. As soon as you leave the room they seem to make it a mission to find out why you like spending so much time there. Unfortunately, this can include nibbling the soft edges off or jumping up on top and trying to burrowing into the cushions. Don't worry you are not the first person to have this problem and there are lots of quite simple bunny proofing things you can do to help stop the damage.

In this guide we have some simple ideas to keep your couch looking neat like throwing a cover over it.

We have ideas on how to protect the legs and other wooden edges that tend to get nibbled using a range of bunny proofing from old toilet roll tubes to tough plastic corner guards.

**Bethany**
When you come downstairs to find this!!! Then catch her in the act AFTER being repacked!!! This momma is not happy right now. Brand new couch set

We also investigate taste deterrents like bitter sprays and how they could help and the best ways to apply them.

Don't wait for your couch to get tatty, try out some of these tried and tested bunny proofing methods and prevent unsightly damage and avoid costly repairs.

## How to keep your couch looking neat

Over time the materials on your couch can start to look tatty due to the extra wear and tier where your bunny sits. The materials can be nibbled or scratched, and the surfaces can be soiled by the odd accident or dirty paws.

An easy way you can provide some protection is by throwing a cover over the top.

It's best to choose a natural material as it may itself be chewed and pick material which can be washed easily or replaced cheaply.

If your bunny does favor a spot on the couch it can be best to turn over this area to them and keep the damage contained by putting a towel down on this spot or a pet bed to take the brunt of the damage.

### How to discipline your bunny for wrecking your couch

- Only tell your bunny off when you catch them playing with your couch or they won't understand why you are being mean to them.
- Even if you bunny is being naughty never hit or push your bunny off the couch, they have small bones that can be hurt easily.
- Never shout at or scare your bunny to get them to stop chewing or digging on your couch, they have sensitive hearing and stress can make them timid or aggressive towards you.

**My girl Isis**
My girl Isis has made a heart shape in the cover lol

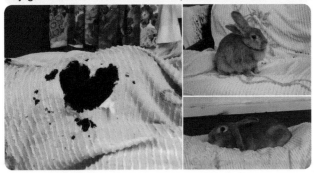

### Did you know

### Bunnies can easily leap three feet off the ground

Rabbits are very good at jumping and climbing and can easily leap onto surfaces a least three feet off the ground. They are constantly on the lookout for food and will explore new places to forage in the hope of finding something tasty.

You may find your bunny will want to explore your couch and will happily jump right up on to the back without any fear or idea of how they will get down.

## Protecting the edges and legs of your couch

A good way to protect the edges around the bottom of your couch is to use a Willow bridges toy that you will find in most pet stores. They are made from a series of willow sticks held together with wire that can be bent into a variety of shapes.

This toy can be bent into an elbow shape to cover the corner and then rested up against it. It can also be bent all the way around a leg to protect it.

Another great way of stopping chewing damage is to build a low fence around your couch which can be done easily with the section of office storage cubes.

Repurposed bunny toys can be used for protection.

These foot square wire grids can be linked together and set out around the base of your couch.

If you want to stop your couch legs being chewed why not try to shield them by slipping them inside some toilet or kitchen roll tubes. Cut the tubes along the length and wrap them around the legs to add a layer of protection.

## Also see

**25** How to stop your bunny chewing your wooden furniture

**Bethany**
I fixed my couch and Bethany yet again found a way! She is so proud

## Using bitter sprays for protect

Bitter sprays can help make the areas around the base of your couch less appealing to chew on however it will probably not stop this unwanted behavior entirely.

It can also be difficult to use on the seating areas and arms without contaminating yourself so is best used alongside other bunny proofing measures.

Remember to keep reapplying the bitter spray regularly so it doesn't lose its effectiveness.

It's best to make under your couch a no-go area to you bunny

Always use a product designed specifically for bunnies and avoid homemade remedies like perfume, soap or chilly oil as these can be harmful to your bunny.

### Also see

**40** Using bitter spray to stop your bunny chewing carpet, wallpaper, baseboards and furniture

### What's the best type of bunny proof couch?

**Double trouble**
I've tried couch covers, sewing, patching, using bitter apple spray (even though she's digging, but I'm desperate!), but nothing seems to work. I've given up re-sewing because I don't want to waste my time to just have her dig it up again!

Lastly if you are considering buying a new couch then making a choice with your bunny in mind can save a lot of the problems for you in the future.

Bunnies love to chew soft materials such as cloth and wood so if you can choose a couch designed with metal feet or an exposed metal frame this will be far more resistant to wear and tear from unwanted chewing.

Bunnies have a natural urge to dig which can cause a lot of damage

Leather or other solid materials will also be a lot tougher and couches that have removable, washable, and even replaceable covers are ideal.

It's best to avoid couches with tassels or skirts that hang down as there will always be a temptation to chew on these.

A leather couch is ideal to stop stains and will not be as appealing to chew.

---

**Bunny proof checklist**
- [x] Cover your couch in a throw to help keep it looking neat.
- [x] Spray on some taste deterrent to make your couch less appealing to chew on.
- [x] Cover wooden legs in toilet roll tubes
- [x] Protect edges from chewing by fencing them off with wood or wire storage grids.

# How to stop your bunny going underneath your couch

## Inside this article

It is natural for your bunny to want to explore and relax in areas around your home that offer shelter.

As a prey species they have strong instincts to look for cover and the underneath of your couch is a place of safety they will return to again and again no matter how many times you fish them out.

Unfortunately, the unfinished material in these out of sight places can contain a number of dangers to an unsuspecting bunny. The flimsy materials are often crudely nailed or stapled together which can cause harm if brushed up against or chewed and digested.

A simple wooden frame be a permanent solution

The plastic material covering the underside can contain long strands of indigestible plastic that can leave your bunny very sick and even needing a costly visit to the vets if eaten.

Many bunny parents have also discovered to their peril that these flimsy covers underneath are not strong enough to stop their bunny breaking through where they have become trapped inside.

This is why many bunny owners choose to make under their couch a no-go area for their bunnies and in this guide show you how you can do this easily by filling the space with some storage.

We also have some examples of how you can use office storage cubes and wooden frames to permanently block access.

Take a look and find an idea that will work for you.

## Some simple ways stop access under your couch

If you are in need of some simple ways to bunny proof under your couch then try some of these ideas commonly used to do the job.

A simplest way to block off access under your couch is by filling in the gap with something that will be resistant to chewing damage and plastic storage boxes are ideal for this.

They are cheap and come in a variety of sizes so you can measure up the gap and find something that fits snugly.

These can then be filled with clothes, toys and shoes which can also help keep them out of your bunnies reach.

**Rex**
My husband built this to protect our chair. So far so good!

If you want something that looks a little less cluttered than using storage boxes or there isn't enough of a gap to usefully fill the space, then a common way of blocking access to this area is to use a few lengths of wood.

These can be cut to size then slid under your couch around the edges to act as a barrier.

Bunnies can be quite strong if they want to move something out the way so make sure the blocks of wood can't easily be moved about by using something substantial or by putting something heavy behind them.

**Block the space under your couch with**

- Some plastic storage boxes
- Lengths of wood
- Cardboard boxes

## How to permanently stop your bunny going underneath your couch

Stop your bunny destroying the underside of your couch, here's how to block this space off!

Underneath your couch can be a dangerous place for a bunny, the materials can be harmful if eaten and there is always the chance your bunny will get stuck inside. Make it permanently off limits with the following bunny proofing ideas.

If you are OK with some home improvement skills then it can be a great idea to make a simple wooden frame to go under your couch.

This works well as it will stay in place if your couch moves about and can provide a solid base if you want to attach some additional bunny proofing around the back.

Another option is to make a fence from sections broken out of some office storage cubes.

These small foot square wire grills can be tied end to end with cable ties and lashed to the legs of your couch with a few bits of string.

These can easily be brought out when your bunny is roaming freely and put away folded away when not needed.

**The dangers to bunnies underneath your couch**

- Unfinished materials, splinters and nails
- Long strands of indigestible string
- Folding mechanisms that can crush your bunny
- Access to the inside where your bunny can get stuck

The safest option is to build a wooden frame under your couch

**Bunny proof checklist**

- [x] Use some storage boxes to fill in the space underneath.
- [x] Fence it off with some office storage grids. These can be lashed to the sides of the bed with cotton string.
- [x] fix some blocks of wooden timber around the edge.
- [x] Move couches with reclining mechanisms out of harm's way in case your bunny gets trapped and hurts themselves.

# How to stop your bunny going behind your couch

### Inside this article

Bunnies often like to explore or even sit in the gap between the wall and the back of your couch. There are good reasons why this should be avoided.

It can lead to chewing damage building up without you noticing which if unchecked can cause quite a lot of damage and even give your bunny access to the inside of the couch where your bunny can get stuck.

Your couch may also not be as static as your bunny imagines and if it moves suddenly when someone sits down it can be pushed back, trapping and hurting them.

It's always best to block off this area before any of these problems occur using one of the following bunny proofing methods.

**Mr Smudge**
What to do when your bun keeps going behind the couch? Build a shelf for him, of course!! I definitely suggest this route as a last resort. We tried everything prior, he's a little shit sometimes.

## Simple ideas to stop your bunny going behind your couch

If you are in need of some simple ways to stop your bunny going behind your couch why not try out some of these commonly used solutions.

To help stop your couch moving about make sure it is pushed back fully up against the wall.

If it's on wheels or can easily slide about you may want to use some coasters to help hold it in place.

Couches are often odd shapes so even if you have pushed it back you may also need to cover the gap that is left between the couch and the walls.

A simple way to do this is with a few well placed sturdy ornaments at each end or by moving some other bits of furniture up against it to cover over the gap.

Another simple solution can be to fill the space with something you want to store away that is resistant to being chewed.

Plastic storage boxes are ideal for this as they are cheap and come in a variety of sizes so you can pack the gap out. They can also be a great way of hiding things away from your bunny like shoes or toys to stop them being chewed.

## Permanent ways to stop your bunny going behind your couch

It is best to find some way to keep your bunny out from behind your couch permanently if you can. Follow these simple ideas other bunny parents use that do the job.

The best way to block access is to cover over the sides. There are many materials you can use including wooden boards cut to shape or sections of pet pen fencing or wire grids.

These can be lashing to the sides with some string or trapped in place by placing a heavy ornament up against them.

It's best to avoid using cardboard as this can easily be chewed through and may prove more of an encouragement.

If you are handy with DIY a permanent solution can be to first build a frame under your couch. This can be used to stop your bunny getting underneath and then to build the sides up to cover the gap by attaching a few bits of wooden board.

Some people go as far as putting a shelf or wooden frame behind the sofa to keep it all boxed in.

# How to make your couch safe for your bunny to play on

**Inside this article**

Bunnies just like other pets like to find their spot on the couch, and just like other pets you have to be mindful of the dangers it can put them in.

Follow this simple guide to learn how you and your family can make sure your couch is a safe place for your bunny to play and relax around.

It includes tips on how to make it a bit safer for your bunny to jump on and off your couch.

Our list of safety rules to guide you and your family when your bunny is around the couch.

We also take a look at what to do if you have a rocking chair or a couch with a relying mechanism and you are worried about your bunnies safety.

**Buddy**
This is what is left from our recliner

Don't take any chances, keep the advice in this guide in mind and keep your couch and bunny safe.

## Check it safe for your bunny to jump on and off your couch

Some bunnies love to jump on and climb about the couch, unfortunately bunnies also tend to leap before the look which can lead to an accident if you are unprepared for this to happen.

Make sure you and your family follow these simple bunny proofing safety rules to avoid mishaps or harm when your bunny comes out.

Bunnies are good climbers and like to jump on the seat and even the back of couches which is why scattering loose cushions can be dangerous if your bunny loses its footing on them and falls.

It's best to keep cushions to a minimum and avoid stacking them up or placing them on the back top or at the front of the seat.

If you have a hard surface under your couch like a wooden floor or tiles, then it's best to try and soften

the landings where your bunny jumps down or may fall by putting a rug down.

This can make it a lot kinder on your bunny's paws but is especially helpful if your bunny has a habit of slipping off the edge of the couch from time to time.

Be careful not to scatter too many cushions as the could cause your bunny to lose its footing

Make sure coffee tables are pushed back and other furniture or ornaments are moved away from the

couches edge so if your bunny does jump or slide off, they won't crash into them on the way down.

## Never leave anything on your couch that your bunny can get to

Bunnies will often leap onto your couch without knowing what is in the way of their landing so it's best to get into the habit of not leaving anything on the seat that could cause harm.

### Snowflake
Who says you need to bunny proof? (They have been working at this for months. We decided to give it to them after the first bite.)

Always keep sharp objects like scissors or knives and folks or glassware off the seat and never put hot food and drink down that could be knocked over as it only takes a second for a situation to unfold and an accident to happen.

Never leave TV remote controls, earphones, phones, books, magazines or bags out on the couch unless you want them to be your bunnies next snack. Not only could this be costly, if it's chewed the materials could also hurt your bunnies tummy if eaten.

You are not alone if your bunny has chewed your remote control

## Make rocking chairs and recliners off limits
No matter how conscientious you are rocking, chairs will always be a danger around an unsuspecting bunny, trapping their feet or crushing them underneath. It is best to place rocking chairs in a room that is off limits.

Couches or armchairs with moving parts such as reclining mechanisms are also unsuitable if your bunny has free roam in a room with them in. Not only can your bunny become trapped in the moving parts and get badly hurt, they can easily find a way inside where they can become stuck and hurt themselves.

Couches or armchairs that have power cables can be dangerous if you bunny chews them and any wires leading up to them will need bunny proofing as well.

---

## Bunny proof checklist
- [x] Don't stack up cushions on your couch which can cause your bunny to fall.
- [x] Never leave sharp objects, glass or hot food or drinks on your couch.
- [x] Soften the landing on hard surfaces where your bunny jumps down with a rug.
- [x] Move rocking chairs to an area where your bunny does not roam freely to avoid accidents.
- [x] Couches or armchairs with moving parts are unsuitable around bunnies that can get trapped and hurt.
- [x] Never leave TV remotes, phones, magazines, or bags out on the couch as they will be chewed.

# How to stop your bunny chewing your wooden furniture

**Inside this article**

If your bunny likes to nibble at your furniture, it's best to put a stop to this before it becomes noticeable. What starts as a few scratches here and there can soon turn into the soft wooded edges being completely rounded off.

In this article we take a look at the damage that can happen to these bits of furniture and show you the ways other bunny parents have found to protect them using a variety of bunny proofing measures.

We have some great tips and tricks to how to protect your table and chair legs that are a common target for unwanted chewing behavior.

Table and chair legs, the soft wooden edges of dressers and sideboards and even laminated wooden cabinets can all be on the menu for a hungry bunny.

We also show you how to set out some simple bunny proofing to keep your furniture out of reach.

If you want to add some permanent protection, we show you what you can do using tough plastic corner guards.

If you think using a taste deterrent like a bitter spray could help, we have details on what's best to use and the best way to apply it.

So if your bunny has decided your furniture is on the menu and you need some practical ways to put a stop to it then continue reading this guide and see what bunny proofing would work best for you.

## How to stop your bunny chewing your furniture legs

If your bunny is in the habit of chewing the legs of your wooden furniture, then there are lots of inventive ways to stop this that people have found, many of which re-purpose bunny toys or other things found around the home.

A simple but clever trick can be to use some toilet or kitchen roll tubes as protection. Either slip over the legs or cut them along the length and wrap them around.

Another useful item that can be purchased from pet stores is a Willow bridge. They are made from a series of willow sticks held together with wire that can

be bent into a variety of shapes or around a table leg to shield it from being chewed.

I wrap cardboard around the legs and zip tie them

Bunnies have a varied diet which includes many things we would normally consider inedible. Unfortunately, many of the materials the furniture in your home is made of is on the menu.

## How to protect the edges and sides of furniture

An easy way to stop chewing is simply to cover the area to add some solid protection. You could try covering a TV cabinet or coffee tables with a cloth cover that trails down to the floor.

Be careful not to place things on top as bunnies have a habit of tugging at things and could pull a heavy object over themselves.

It can be helpful to rest something up against the sides or a corner. A willow bridge toy is ideal for this as they are heavy enough to not be knocked over and can be bent around the corner to protect it.

Always provide lots of chewing alternatives

We would avoid using cardboard to protect furniture as it does not take long for a bunny to chew through and it may even encourage them to go to this spot when they fancy chewing something.

If you want to be sure your bunny cannot get to a valuable piece of furniture, then it is best to fence off the area with a few sections of pet pen or office storage cubes.

These sections of wire grid can be lashed together with some cable ties or string and made into a fence that can screen off the area.

## Permanent ways of protecting your furniture

Use tough corner guards to add protection

If you are looking for a permanent solution why not install some tough plastic corner guards.

You may have seen these L shaped lengths of tough plastic in public buildings and you can pick them up yourself in most DIY stores.

They can be easily cut to size with a craft knife and can be attached with some sticky pads or adhesive, so you don't need any DIY Skills to install them.

### Using taste deterrents

#### Kugel

So our bunny is exhibiting new behaviors. She finally figured out how to jump on our dining room chairs (which is fine) and now she spends hours just hanging out there and constantly licking the fabric. She's even been sleeping on the chair through the night.

Bitter sprays can help make wooden furniture, chair or table legs a little less appealing to chew on however, most people discover they don't offer a single solution to a chewing problem and need to be used alongside other bunny proofing.

You can apply the spray directly to the affected area or to help stop the spray going everywhere you can also spray some into a cloth then wipe the liquid on.

### Miss Nibbles and the Mr Biscuit
When your shoes have been safe at this level for months and months and months. And suddenly they are not! Protection deployed !!!!!

Remember to keep reapplying the bitter spray regularly so it does not lose its effectiveness.

Avoid home-made remedies that may be suggested to you such as perfume or chilly oil as these can be harmful to your bunny.

We would also avoid remedies such as double-sided sticky tape that could get stuck in your bunnies fur or cause problems if eaten. Instead choose a product designed for bunnies.

### How to tell your bunny off for chewing your wooden furniture

- Only tell your bunny of when you catch them chewing your furniture or they won't understand why you are being mean to them.
- Even if you bunny is being naughty and chews your furniture, never hit or shove your bunny away as they can be hurt very easily.

- Never shout at or scare your bunny to get them to stop chewing something they shouldn't. Causing them stress can make them antisocial towards you.
- Always provide lots of hay and chew toys to give them something else to eat other than your furniture.

### Also see

**40** Using bitter spray to stop your bunny chewing carpet, wallpaper, baseboards and furniture

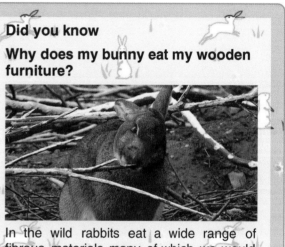

**Did you know**

**Why does my bunny eat my wooden furniture?**

In the wild rabbits eat a wide range of fibrous materials many of which we would not consider to be edible.

Unfortunately, many of the wooden or cloth materials furniture your home is made of is ideal for helping your bunnies digestion and to wear down their teeth that unlike our teeth grow constantly throughout their lives.

### Bunny proof checklist
- [x] Temporarily protect furniture by leaning a ceramic tile or a willow bridge up against them.
- [x] Protect table and chair legs from chewing damage by slipping some toilet roll tube over them,
- [x] Protect the edges of furniture from being chewed with plastic corner guards available from a DIY stores,
- [x] Using taste deterrents to help make your wooden furniture less appealing,
- [x] Use some pet pen or office storage grids to fence of furniture,

# How to stop your bunny eating your house plants

It only takes your back to be turned for a second for one of your house plants to be mowed down or stripped of its bark by a hunger bunny.

It is essential to bunny proof your house plants, not only is this frustrating if they are eaten it can also be harmful as many plants can be toxic to bunnies.

In this guide we show you some great ways other bunny parents have found to keep their plants out of reach and safe.

And we show you some of the hidden dangers that can harm your bunny.

Don't take any chances, follow this guide to make sure you can relax with your bunny out safely.

That moment that you realize that your rabbits have been eating your favorite plant

## Dangers to look out for

Plants in reach can be easily tugged over

It's unlikely you are going to be able to teach your bunny not to chew your plants, the best way to bunny proof them is to move them out of harm's way by either placing them on a shelf or piece of furniture that cannot be reached by your bunny.

Make sure your plant is on something solid so your bunny cannot topple it over and be careful of table clothes that trail down as bunnies have a habit of tugging at things and could pull the plant over itself.

The soil can also contain materials that could be saturated with chemicals that can be harmful if eaten so you should make this off limits.

It's also important that your bunny can't get to the water as this can be contaminated with plant food or pesticides which are toxic.

If you water your plants from the base, make sure this cannot be reached as this can also be harmful to your bunny if they try to drink the water as it can be contaminated with plant food.

Falling leaves can also be a potential danger so always ensure that if they were to fall, they would fall into an area that also can't be reached.

### Harvey

I forgot to bunny proof. I've been letting Harvey into our master bedroom and then I recently started letting him free roam at night as well. I forgot to move my violet to my bedroom window sill which is totally at bunny height. He's fine btw.

Bunnies are great climbers so always check there are no overhanging branches that can be reached and there is no way you bunny can get to the plant indirectly.

If it's a larger plant that's on the floor you can also fence it off with a few sheets taken from a pet pen.

Make sure plants you don't want eaten are kept out of reach

## Ashes

Soooooo ... We had a brief scare today because Ashes chewed the leaf of an orchid that I laid on the floor while moving more stuff into my new place. The vet suggested filing a claim with the Pet Poison Hotline, which I did, and no issues really. Good info for future emergencies however.

## What to do if you think your bunny has eaten a toxic plant

- Check the ASPCA toxic plants for more information and work out how much your bunny has eaten.
- Signs that your bunny has eaten something include a loss in appetite, seizures, lethargy, hunching, problems breathing, discharge from nose, gassy and painful abdomen.
- Don't panic. Many poisonous plants to rabbits can be consumed in small amounts with little to no problems

- However never wait if you think there is a problem, contact a vet straight away for help

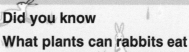

### Did you know
### What plants can rabbits eat

A wild rabbit is normally quite safe munching on the abundance of plants they are familiar with in their environment.

However, the colorful and exotic plants you may have in your home can often be very poisonous to an unsuspecting bunny. Sadly, your bunny may not recognize a plant is toxic by its taste.

Bunnies love digging in things and if you don't keep your plant pots out of reach, they will always be tempted to play in them

## Bunny proof checklist

- [X] Many house plants are poisonous to bunnies, make sure they are out of reach and check to make sure your bunny can't climb and stretch to get to them
- [X] Don't place plant pots or flower vases near the edge of furniture tops in case it's knocked over or pulled off as this can hurt your bunny if it falls on them
- [X] Don't let your bunny drink the water from watering trays or dig in the soil which can contain harmful chemicals like pesticides and fertilizer

# How to make your yard safe and secure for your bunny

## Inside this article

Before you let your bunny roam freely in your yard it's important to do some bunny proofing first. Bunnies are curious creatures and can find their way into trouble. In this guide we show you how to do a quick sweep of your garden and what to watch out for that may be dangerous.

Bunnies are also excellent diggers and can easily find their way out from under a fence so we also show you how to fully fence off the perimeter to avoid escapes. Finally we discuss the dangers and solutions for keeping your bunnies safe from wild as well as domestic predators.

There can be a lot of things to keep in mind so follow this practical guide to learn step by step how to do all the essential bunny proofing jobs in your yard.

**Gwyneth**
I give up!

## How to protect your bunny from predators in your yard

Foxes can lift up a wooden framed bunny runs and chew through chicken wire

If you let a house bunny roam in your yard there is always the danger of attack from wild and domestic predators. If you are worried about this, pet stores sell many types of runs and pens you can purchase.

Make sure they offer protection from the top and are secured to the ground. Predators like foxes can easily lift up and get under a light, wooden framed bunny run or even chew through thin chicken wire.

## Always do a quick safety sweep to make sure it's safe

Every time you let your bunny out do a quick sweep to check things through. Look for anything that could be knocked over and fall on your bunny which could hurt it. Store away anything that is stacked up or leaning against a wall like a broom or shovel.

Also be careful not to leave bicycles lent up against a wall as bunnies can become entangled in the chain or even knock it over causing it to fall on them.

Make sure all chemicals such as fertilizers, weed killers, insecticides or cleaning agents are stored out of reach on a high shelf or in a locked cupboard.

They are not only harmful if your bunny was to accidentally eat them, they may also cause harm if they get them on their fur.

The water as it can be contaminated with plant food which could be harmful to your bunny if they try and drink it.

If you water your plants from the base, make sure the watering trays can't be reached.

### Remember to regularly check the perimeter for escape routes

**Myrtle**
Can anyone tell me what's wrong in this picture?

The perimeter of your yard will constantly be tested by your exploring bunny. They can crawl through surprisingly small gaps and with a bit of digging and chewing they can quickly open up a space big enough to squeeze through. Here are a few things to check to make sure you have bunny proofed all the escape routes.

Don't take any chances, even if your fence goes down to the ground it's best to dig along the edge and bury some bricks or lengths of wood along the edge.

If you have a hedge then you will need to add some additional reinforcement. You can make it escape proof with some wire mesh, it is best to bury this into the ground so it can't be undermined. If your bunny starts to excavate a spot try laying a paving stone over the area can stop it.

Gates often have a space underneath them which although seems small is big enough for a bunny to crawl under. Block off any spaces under or around the gate.

If the gate does not close on its own, fit a self-closing mechanism to make sure it keeps shut.

### How to keep your bunny out of your flower bed or garden

Bunnies like to try just about anything at least once to see if it can be eaten. Sharp teeth can strip bark from trees or shrubs.

Flower beds can make a tasty treat and soil can be dug up and young roots eaten. If you have a flower bed or garden area with vegetables in it, you will need to protect these areas to stop your bunny helping themselves.

Just about the only way you can keep your bunny out is to fence an area in or fence off a smaller area for your bunny to play in. A pet pen can be used on its own or broken up to make a fence.

If you have any trees that overhang your garden it is worth considering that some trees have berries or leaves that may be toxic that could fall into your yard. Make sure you clear these away.

### What to do if you think your bunny has eaten a toxic plant in your yard

Firstly don't panic, many plants in your yard that are listed as poisonous to rabbits can be consumed in small amounts however, never wait if you think there is a problem, contact a vet straight away for help.

Its best to work out what the plant is and how much your bunny has eaten then check the ASPCA toxic plants list for more information.

Signs that your bunny has eaten something include a loss in appetite, seizures, lethargy, hunching, problems breathing, discharge from nose, gassy and painful abdomen.

---

**Bunny proof checklist**

- [x] Make sure all chemical such as fertilizers, weed killers, insecticides or cleaning agents are stored out of reach
- [x] Put away anything that could be knocked over and fall on your bunny like a shovel or bicycle
- [x] Make sure watering trays cannot be drank from as they can be contaminated with plant food
- [x] Check the perimeter fencing, hedges and gates regularly for escape routes.

# How to stop your bunny escaping from your yard

If you let your bunnies free roam in your yard then you need to check constantly that they are not planning an escape.

Follow this guide to see how other bunny parents secure their yard so you can relax without worrying.

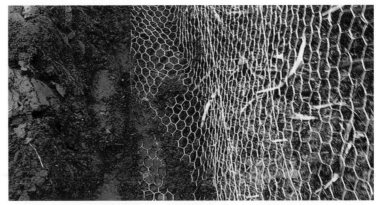

Bury the fence into the ground to stop it being undermined

## Always check for new escape tunnels

Bunnies like to explore their surroundings and will spend time around the edges of your yard where they feel safe. It's natural for them to shape their habitat by digging and chewing and can quickly open up a space under a fence or through a hedge big enough to squeeze through.

Even if your fence goes down to the ground bunnies can quickly excavate a hole big enough for them to squeeze through.

A sure way to stop this is to bury something under the fence like a line of bricks or another piece of wooden fencing.

A great way to stop your bunny digging is simply to lay a paving stone over the spot where you want to stop it.

If you have a hedge, then the best way to make it escape proof is to use some wire mesh. Make sure you bury it a bit into the ground so it can't be undermined.

Back gates nearly always need some improvement and it's especially important to bunny proof them if they lead to dangers outside such as a busy street or areas where people walk their dogs. Extend the gate so there is no space below the bottom of the gate and the ground.

Gates with self-closing mechanisms are ideas to help you get in and out easily and with other family members and guests who may not be initiated in stopping bunnies escaping.

Remember the edge of your yard will constantly be tested by your bunny so make sure you check regularly to see if an escape route is developing under a hedge or behind some furniture.

### Did you know

### Why does my bunny keep trying to escape from my yard?

Rabbits like to explore and it's in their nature to try and take advantage of the environment to find the best food and shelter. They are always testing their boundaries to see what they can find.

Even if you give your bunny everything they need they will try and escape as the grass will always seem greener on the other side of the fence.

# How to stop your bunny chewing your doors and door frames

**Inside this article**

The soft wooden edges of your doors and door frames make an easy target for a bored bunny and it only takes a few nibbles for the damage to be noticeable. Over time a bunny on a mission can eventually do a lot of damage, costing a lost deposit or expensive repairs. If you want to keep your doors and door frames looking neat, then here are some simple ideas other bunny moms use to stop chewing damage.

**Bear**
Yet again that oaf has destroyed my day!

## Easy temporary protection

Easy bunny proofing that can be easily packed away when not needed

If your bunny is repeatedly chewing your door frames the simplest way to provide temporary protection is to lay something up against the areas when you bunny is showing interest.

Ceramic tiles or willow bridges, a toy found in pet stores, are ideal for this. They can then be easily packed away when not needed.

A well placed cardboard box or chew toy can also make a great distraction.

### Protect your doors frames using tough corner guards

A simple way to protect fragile edges along the base of a door or on your door frames is to use a cheap commercial product designed specifically to stop this type of damage.

You may have seen these L shaped lengths of tough plastic in public buildings and you can buy them in most home improvement stores and fit them yourself.

They come in a variety of lengths however if you need to cut down to size this can be done with a craft knife so no need for any DIY tools.

They can then be easily attached with some sticky pads or adhesive. They come in a wood color, white and clear so you will be able to match it with the door.

### How should I tell my bunny off for chewing my doors

- Even if you bunny is being naughty, never hit or shove your bunny away as they can be hurt very easily.
- Don't keep your bunny quiet with treats, you may be teaching them bad behavior.
- Never shout at or scare your bunny to get them to stop chewing your doors or frames. Stress can make them antisocial towards you.

### Fitting an acrylic cover or kick plate could save your door from chewing

Another common type of damage can be caused by your bunny stripping off the soft wood laminate from the bottom edge of the door. A solid way of stopping this is to install a Kick plate.

Although this will require some home improvement skills it will fix the problem and will save your replacing the door.

### Using bitter sprays

**Cooper**

Hi does anyone have any advice on how to stop my bunny from chewing my door? As you can see clear tape & brown tape haven't deterred him nor has the no chew spray I bought?

Bitter sprays can help make the corners of doors and door frames a lot less appealing to your bunny to chew however, bunnies transform their environment by chewing it and may be prepared to put up with the taste if they really feel the urge to chew a door.

If you think taste deterrent will help, follow these simple steps to apply it the best way.

You can apply the spray directly to the affected area or to help stop the spray going everywhere you can also spray some into a cloth then wipe the liquid on.

Remember to keep reapplying the bitter spray regularly so it doesn't lose its effectiveness.

Avoid homemade remedies like perfume or chilly oil as these can be harmful to your bunny and instead use a product designed for bunnies.

We would also avoid remedies such as double-sided sticky tape that could get stuck in your bunnies fur or cause problems if eaten.

**Did you know**

**Why does my bunny chew my door frames**

Bunnies communicate using their teeth and make a variety of noises from gentle tooth clicks when they are happy to full tantrums where they like to pick things up and bash them about.

They can easily learn that the sound of them chewing a door will get you up and get them attention.

---

**Bunny proof checklist**

- [x] Temporarily protect door frames from being chewed by leaning a ceramic tile up against them.
- [x] Protect the soft wooden corners of your door frames by fitting some plastic corner guards.
- [x] Apply some bitter spray to areas being chewed to act as a deterrent.
- [x] Install a bunny gates to rooms you need to control access to. It will make it easier to come and go and help prevent breakouts.

# Why pet gates are the ultimate bunny proofing hack

**Inside this article**

When you live with a house bunny there are going to be times when you need to restrict access to a room or through a doorway to your bunny. This is where many bunny parents have discovered using a pet gate can come in very handy.

In this guide we show you how a bunny gate can be used to help make areas of your home off limits, like a kitchen where your bunny could get underfoot, a bedroom where you bunny has a habit of peeing on your bed or a door leading outside to prevent an escape.

We also have a guide to the different types of bunny gate and how people have modified them with mesh to stop their bunnies sneaking through them.

**Stew, Shadow and Willow**
I made my own using burlap lol it's what I had at my house and it's worked so far.

## What the best sort of pet gate to use for a bunny

**George**
We personalised George's gate - as you can tell, he's very impressed.

You can pick up a pet gate from any pet store. They are relatively cheap and can be installed without modifying your home or the need for home improvement skills.

Make sure you use something designed for pets as although baby gates are similar the bars can be spaced out wide enough for a small bunny to squeeze through.

Try and find one that locks in an open as well as a closed position as this can help when you want your bunny to come in and out.

## The reasons pet gates are so good when you have a bunny

Pet gates are a definite help when you have a free roaming bunny. With a pet gate you can leave the door open to an area where your bunny is and still keep an eye on them. This can also help stop your bunny getting frustrated listening to you in the next room which can lead to them chewing and scratching at the door and any chewing will instead be taken out on the gate.

If you have every opened a door on your bunnies paws you will know how bad this can make you feel so being able to see your bunny through a pet gate before you go into a room can make coming and going easier as bunnies do have a habit of sitting the other side of a door if they hear you coming.

They are especially helpful with family members or guests that are not familiar with bunnies as they automatically swing shut preventing breakouts.

# How to stop your bunny chewing your curtain and blinds

## Inside this article

It can be very frustrating if your bunny starts eating your curtains or blinds. They can do quite a lot of damage when left in a room on their own.

Bunnies have razor sharp teeth which grow constantly throughout their lives so are always looking for something to chew on to wear them down and can make short work of cloth and even the tough material lateral blinds are made of. Other damage can include chewing the end of drawstrings and tassels which can be cleanly sliced off in seconds.

In this guide we show you the many ways other long suffering bunny parents have found to limit the damage to their curtains and keep them out of harm's reach.

**Ozric**
I would definitely not bother with floor length curtains again

We also have a few safety ideas you should take note of around drawstrings and synthetic materials.

And if you think it would help, we have a guide to what the best taste deterrent is to use and how best to apply them.

Don't wait for your bunny to take your curtains up, follow these remedies and avoid expensive repairs.

## How to bunny proof where your curtains get chewed

Draw the curtains in a bit from the end wall out of your bunnies way

Curtain chewing is a common problem with house bunnies and you are lucky if your bunny is not tempted to chew them. You will often find that the worst of the damage can occur at each end of the curtains. This may be the spot where your bunny likes to run along behind them then pop in and out. If you draw the curtains in a bit from the end wall your bunny will not see them as in its way and hopefully ignore them.

A way of protecting the curtains to avoid any chance of damage is to fence them off with sections taken from a pet pen. These can be set out free standing so are an easy way to make a bunny no go area.

If you want something you can quickly and easily bring out to add protection and act as a distraction try putting a tunnel toy or cardboard box there to keep the curtains pulled back and out of the way.

Hopefully, you bunny will want to chew this more than your curtains when they pass by.

## Did you know

### Why does my bunny chew my curtains and blinds

Rabbits like to maintain their habitats and adapt them to their individual needs. Bit by bit they can chew their surrounding into shape and have razor sharp teeth that can easily slice through tough roots and shoots.

If your curtains stand in their way over time this damage will build up leaving you with costly repairs unless you keep them out of the way.

## Keep curtain drawstrings out of reach

Bunnies can get tangled up in drawstrings and hurt

Always keep drawstrings or other cords out of reach, not only could they be an easy target for chewing your bunny may get tangled up in them and hurt itself.

If you don't have a regular way of doing this, then install a hook and make tying it up out of reach a habit when your bunny is roaming in the room.

Always keep an eye on how much cord your bunny is eating. Synthetic material can be hard to digest for and if you catch your bunny eating too much it could make them unwell.

### Bunny safety tips for curtains and blinds

- Make sure loops are kept out of reach so your bunny does not get tangled up in them.
- Don't let your bunny eat the synthetic materials as it can bind up their tummies
- Be careful of your bunny rushing out and getting underfoot. You may be best to fence this area off.

## Applying bitter sprays

Bitter sprays can be helpful if you are battling to stop your bunny chewing your curtains or blinds but it sometimes only offers a partial solution as you may find your bunny more than prepared to put up with a bad taste.

As always, it's a combination of bunny proofing things that will prove most effective.

Apply the spray on the area being chewed and any other areas that look like they could be a target as well. Remember to reapply regularly so it doesn't lose its effectiveness.

Avoid home-made remedies such as as perfume, soap or chilly oil.

These can be harmful to your bunny and instead use a product designed for bunnies.

## Also see

**40** Using bitter spray to stop your bunny chewing carpet, wallpaper, baseboards and furniture

### Bunny proof checklist

- [x] Damage can occur at each end where your bunny pops in and out, try drawing your curtains in a bit at the ends to keep the path clear.
- [x] Make your curtains a lot less appealing to chew on with taste deterrents like a bitter spray.
- [x] Consider taking your curtains up before your bunny does this for you.
- [x] Always provide lots of chew toys to keep your bunny occupied and a stack of hay to eat each day.

# How to bunny proof your bed

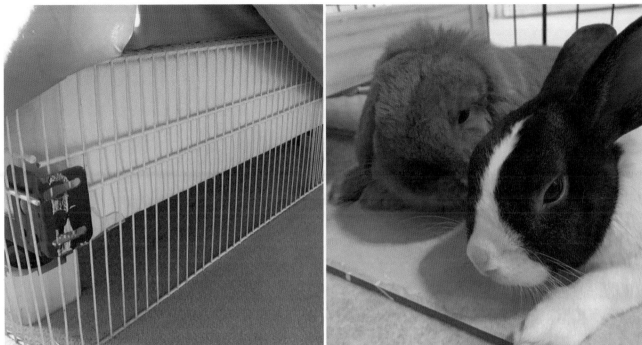

If your bunny has access to your bed it can turn into a bit of a battle to share this space. Unwanted naughty behaviour can include nibbling the soft edges of wooden bed frame or materials that hang down around the edges or underneath. This can cause a lot of damage over time and keep you awake at night.

If you are having any of these or other problems don't worry you are not alone.

In the guide we show you the ways other bunny parents have bunny proofed their bed to block the space underneath.

We also show you how to use gentle discipline without causing stress.

## How to stop your bunny going under your bed

There are many reasons why you may want to restrict access under your bed to your bunny. Bunnies have a habit of chewing materials that hang down over the sides and tugging at the covers underneath which can cause quite a lot of damage to your sheets and mattress.

They can even eat the soft wooden edges of your bed itself leaving them splintered and looking tatty.

The spaces under your bed are also unsuitable for bunnies to play in. It can contain unfinished surfaces with nails or splinters and synthetic materials that could cause tummy problems if eaten.

These problems can also be more of a nuisance as well if you sleep in the same room as your bunny and they can keep you awake as they can be active at different times to us.

Fencing under the bed is often the best and simplest way of bunny proofing it

The most common solution to this problem is to make this space off limits and here we point out the benefits of the various solutions people use.

## Quick and easy ways to fill the space under your bed

A quick way to block off the space under your bed is to place some plastic storage tubs underneath it, they are cheap and come in a variety of heights so if you measure the gap before you go to buy them you can get some that fit snugly.

## Fencing in and blocking off the space under your bed

A more permanent solution to stopping your bunny playing under your bed is to place some lengths of wood around the edges. If you are feeling handy you can join these together into a simple frame to make it more secure and stop it moving about.

Another way of blocking access is to use sections of wire storage grids. These can be tied together and lashed to the legs and bed frame with some string or cable ties to secure them.

### Problems with bunnies going under your bed

- Bunnies have different sleep patterns to us so may keep you awake
- There may me unfinished materials under your bed like nails and staples
- Synthetic materials can be bad for bunnies if they eat it
- You bunny may chew the sheets and mattress
- Your bunny may even chew the soft wooden bed and carpet underneath
- They can start a new toilet spot under the bed

## Fencing part of a room off is sometimes the easiest option

If you want to keep your bunny completely away from your bed then sometimes its easier to section off half a room than try and bunny proof everything.

This can be done by taking a pet pen and breaking it up into sheets and using these as a fence. If you lay the out in a zigzag pattern it will help it stand up. You can get fences with a gate in them which will save you climbing over it all the time.

These can then easily be packed away when your bunny is not roaming freely.

## Covering the underside of the bed

If you want to stop your bunny getting to the underside of your bed but don't want the bunny proofing to be obvious an alternative approach can be to board the underside of the bed. Pet pens, wire storage grids or even wooden boards can be used to do this.

You should avoid using cardboard for bunny proofing as this may just encourage your bunny and wont last in the long run.

**Did you know**

**Does my bunny sleep at night**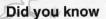

People mistakenly think bunnies are nocturnal or think they will sleep at night when they do, however rabbits are not nocturnal nor do they sleep at night, they're in fact crepuscular. which means they're active at dawn and again at dusk.

This can mean your bunny can wake you up nice and early in the morning in the summertime.

---

**Bunny proof checklist**

- [x] Fill the space with plastic storage tubs.
- [x] Fence around the edge with wire grids.
- [x] Place lengths of wood around the edge to block the gap
- [x] Fence the part of the room off with some sections of pet pen.

# How to use bitter sprays to stop your bunny chewing everything

**Inside this article**

Taste deterrents or bitter sprays can help stop your bunnies unwanted chewing. Most people find they help but don't stop the problem completely and some people's bunnies don't seem to mind the taste.

If you do think it will help then follow this guide where we show you how best to apply the bitter stray and where to use it to get the most from it.

We also have suggestions on what to use and not use as some home remedies can be harmful to your bunny.

Taste deterrents can help stop your bunny chewing

## How best to apply bitter spray

Taste deterrents can be a helpful tool if you are trying to teach your bunny to stop chewing your furniture. To get the most from it the first thing to do is identify all the areas where you think your bunny is going to chew and cover them all in spray so that you don't simply move the problem along to another spot.

Doing this proactively will also help prevent habit forming from the start.

If you want greater control over what is covered then it can be helpful to spray the liquid on to a cloth first, then wipe it on the areas you want.

Do not use the spray around electrical cables or TV screens and try and avoid saturating surfaces with the spray.

Remember it is important to reapply the spray regularly so it remains effective and keep a close eye for damage as some bunnies are more than happy to put up with the taste.

### Where to use bitter spray to stop bunny chewing damage

- The corners and edges of wooden furniture
- Wooden table and chair legs
- Doors, door frames and baseboards
- Curtains and blinds
- Areas of carpet that are being chewed

## What to use as a taste deterrent?

We would only suggest using a bitter spray designed specifically for bunnies or small animals and we would not recommend using home-made alternatives you may have heard about such as chili, clove oil or perfume.

Bitter sprays can be purchased from most pet stores or on-line and typically come in the form of a pump spray or aerosol containing a liquid that is designed to have an unpleasant taste.

Although bitter sprays can help prevent some chewing, the natural urge for a bunny to explore its environment by nibbling a bit here and a bit there can be very hard to stop.

It's always best to do some bunny proofing as well and provide lots of alternative chewing toys alongside areas that may be chewed to keep your bunny out of trouble.

### What NOT TO USE as a taste deterrent for bunnies

- Soap, perfume or scented oils, these are all unsuitable
- Double sided sticky tape, this can get stuck in your bunnies fur
- Chilly oil can make you bunny very uncomfortable and not necessarily stop them

# Top 8 best bunny proofing hacks

Take a look at these Top 8 bunny proofing hacks to find out how you could be making your life easier.

## 1) Split length tubing

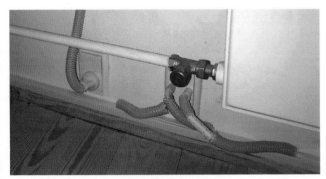

Protect wires in tough Split length tubing

One of the most important bunny proofing jobs you can do is to protect the electrical wires that trail around your home from being chewed. It only takes a moment for your bunnies razor sharp teeth to cut through the soft plastic and serious harm to be done.

A cheap and simple way to protect wires is by slipping them inside some split length tubing which is basically tough plastic piping cut along its length. You can get this pipe from most home improvement stores.

To install it first cut the tubing to the correct length then cut the tubing along its length. Next simply slip the wire inside via the split. You don't even need to take the plug off.

### Also see

③  How to stop your bunny chewing electrical cables

## 2) Backyard escapes

Bury the fence into the ground to stop it being undermined

If you give your bunny access to your garden or yard, then you need to bunny proof the perimeter to stop escapes. Bunnies are good at digging so you will need to extend fencing into the ground by burying wooden boards or a line of bricks below the fence line to prevent escapes.

### 3) Stop chewing damage to carpet and baseboards with an old ceramic tile

A heavy ceramic tile can be a great way of adding some quick and easy bunny proofing protection.

Place the tile over areas of carpet to stop your bunny chewing it.

Lean the tile up against baseboards to protect the soft wood.

### 4) Build a digging box for your bunny

Bunnies love to dig and forage for treats so by making a digging box you can let them have lots of fun and keep them out of trouble at the same time.

You will need a cardboard box big enough to contain the mess but low enough for your bunny to jump into. Next fill it with shredded paper, old toilet roll tubes and anything else they may like.

### Good things to put on a digging box

- Shredded paper
- Straw
- Twigs
- Chew toys

### Also see

69  How to build a digging box for your bunny

### 5) Storage boxes are idea for blocking spaces under furniture

Bunnies love to explore narrow spaces and it's surprising how small a gap they can squeeze through. It is important to block off access to these crawl spaces behind or under furniture where dangerous unfinished materials like nails and staples could hurt your bunny.

A simple way to make an area no go is to fill it with some storage boxes.

A simple way to do this is by filling the space with some plastic storage boxes. This can also be a great way of keeping things you don't want chewed safe. Measure the gap first so you get a snug fit.

### Also see

**20**    How to stop your bunny going underneath your couch

## 6) Repurpose pet toys as bunny protection

Some extra protection by using a willow bridge toy for bunny proofing

Bunnies like to chew on soft wooded material. They chew it to wear down their teeth and can even choose to eat wood as a source of roughage in their diet.

It can be impossible to keep an eye on your bunny all the time and it only takes a moment for noticeable damage to be done if they decide your coffee table or door frames are on the menu, but you can limit the damage.

A simple way to protect these areas from being nibbled on is to deploy some extra protection by shielding and there are lots of bunny toys that you can use such as hideaways or tubes. Willow bridges are also great for covering corners and table legs as they can be bent into a variety of shapes to suit your needs.

## 7) Make a fence with section of pet pen

**Gwyneth**
Hoppy Bunny Butt to all you Rabbit loverrrrrrrs

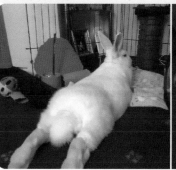

If you want to be sure your bunny is not going to get to a valuable piece of furniture or an area with lots of power cords such as a computer desk it can be easier to fence off the area with a few sections of pet pen.

These sections of wire grid can be lashed together with cable ties and made into a fence that can screen part of a room.

You can set them out as a free-standing fence in a zigzag pattern or lash them to the sides of a piece of furniture with some string. Some bunny moms even go as far as building a perimeter around a room to keep their bunny from reaching the wallpaper and baseboards which can often be a target for unwanted chewing behavior.

## 8) Keep your bunny in a constant supply of chew toys by recycling toilet roll tubes

Bunnies are always looking for something new to chew on however, the novelty of a new chew toy can run out quickly. An easy way to keep your bunny occupied is to repurpose your toilet roll tubes when the roll ends.

From simply stacking them up so your bunny can knock them down and toss them around to snuffing them with hay and hanging them down with bits of string the toys you can make are only limited by your imagination.

To help give you some ideas we have made a load of toilet roll toys and tried them out on our bunny to see what he thought of them. In this guide we show you step by step how we built them and give you our bunnies opinion of what he thought of them.

# Bringing a bunny home for the first time

When you bring a bunny home for the first time there is some simple bunny proofing you need to do to make your home safe and help stop some of the damage from normal chewing behavior.

In this guide for first time bunny parents we cover some of the safety basics such as how best to protect electrical cables as well as lots of tips and tricks to prevent damage to carpet, wallpaper, baseboards and other parts of your home.

Don't wait for a problem to start, learn from others experience what to do and make sure your home is bunny proofed.

Everything you need to know about bringing home a bunny

## Setting up an indoor enclosure

The first thing you will need to organize is a pen. This will be the place your bunny will spend time when you don't want them roaming freely or when they are unsupervised for instance when you are at work or at night when you are in bed.

It needs to be a safe and secure place so you can be certain your bunny will not come to any harm.

It should be large enough for them to stretch and exercise in and contain all the things they need such as food, water, a litter tray and various toys to keep them occupied.

There are lots of types of indoor bunny enclosures that people use so it's a matter of picking the one you think will suit your bunny.

This will also be the best place to start litter training which is essential if you are going to keep house bunnies.

### Also see

**61**  How to build a bunny enclosure

**63**  What should I put in my bunny enclosure?

## Making electrical cables safe for your bunny

Bunnies find chewing wires irresistible, no matter how many times you tell them NO.

They have razor sharp teeth that can cut through the soft insulation in seconds leading to a nasty, even fatal accident which is why bunny proofing the wires in your home is one of the first and most important jobs you need to do before you can let your bunny roam freely.

This may seem a daunting task at first however it only needs doing once and with a bit of time and ingenuity it is possible to make your home 100% safe by either moving wires out of reach by tucking them behind furniture.

Exposed wires can be protected using split length tubing or creating fenced off areas such as behind your TV.

Hide wires in split length tubing

### Also see

**3**  How to stop your bunny chewing electrical cables

## What to do when you bunny chews your carpet

Bunnies love chewing and digging and it's very common for some damage to occur to carpeted areas.

If unchecked this can lead to a significant amount of damage, costly repairs or a loss of deposit.

What's more, the constant distraction of having to jump up and stop this behavior can spoil the time you are supposed to be spending relaxing and enjoying their companionship.

There is no one solution to stopping carpet chewing however there are lots of tips and tricks people use that can help.

The first thing to do is find ways of covering areas that are getting unwanted attention, this can range from putting some cardboard boxes in the areas or covering them over with a rug.

Ceramic tiles are also a quick and easy way to add some temporary protection. It will hold down loose carpet and keep it out of reach. Always provide lots of acceptable digging and chewing alternatives so your bunny can exercise this natural behavior.

Making a digging box can be an excellent alternative and grass mats that can be purchased from pet stores are good for keeping your bunny out of trouble.

### How to stop your bunny chewing wooden furniture, doors and baseboards

if your bunny can play under your bed it can keep you up at night.

Anything made of wood in your home is likely to be chewed at least once. The soft wooden corners of furniture, doors and skirting board can be irresistible to a bunny who will enjoy chewing and even eating the material. Although not typically harmful it can leave your home looking tatty and it's best to try and put a stop to this habit wherever it starts.

Bitter spray or other deterrents can make wood a little less appealing to chew however it works best alongside other bunny proofing measures. Always

use a spray made for pets as many of the home remedies such as soap, vinegar, chilly oil and perfume may be harmful to your bunny.

The only way to really stop the damage is to cover areas in some way and an easy way to do this is to fence it off. In the case of baseboards, products such as office storage cubes can be used. These kits made of 1 foot square of wire grids can be repurposed, broken up and used as a fence along your baseboards to protect them.

Areas where you have a lot of furniture can be totally screened off using larger sections of pet pens set out as a fence.

If you want to add protection to the soft wooden edges of door frames and baseboards you could cover them with plastic corner guards.

Block off the space under your bed with storage boxes

### How to make your couch bunny proofed

Your sofa can become a center of attention for your bunny so its important to make sure it's safe.

As a first step you and your family members will need to learn to avoid placing hot food or sharp objects on the arms or seat.

Bunnies have a habit of jumping up without looking which can lead to a nasty shock. Also make sure you are careful not to pile up too many loose cushions as these can cause your bunny to lose its footing and slip off.

To improve safety further it is sensible to block off access underneath your sofa as it may have unfinished materials like nails, staples and rough wooden edges that can cause harm.

A real problem can occur if your bunny crawls inside which is not only dangerous but can lead to you dismantling your couch to free them.

Lastly, it's best to avoid chairs with reclining mechanisms and rocking chairs altogether, bunnies can gain access to these or become trapped in them and get badly hurt.

### Truffles
This face may look innocent, but this is the face of evil, trusted them to run around outside of their run and come back to find truffles has chewed straight through their BunnyCam cable. Wire? No, just spicy hay.

## Make sure your plants are bunny safe

Unfortunately your bunny will not be able to tell whether a plant is good to eat or not and is likely to want to try so it's important to make sure you move all the plants in your home well out of reach and harm's way.

Make sure that falling leaves don't end up in areas where your bunny can roam also, and remember bunnies are good climbers so make sure they can find a way indirectly.

It's also important that your bunny can't get to the watering tray where it may drink from the water as this can be contaminated with plant food or pesticides which are toxic.

## Safety in the backyard

If your bunny can access outdoor spaces, you will definitely need to bunny proof it. The first concern is preventing escape, make sure you block off gaps in hedges and under fences and gates.

Always do routine checks of the perimeter looking behind bushes or anywhere your bunny can tunnel without you noticing. You may need to bury your bunny proofing into the ground. Also look for anything that could be knocked over and fall on your bunny like a broom shovel or bicycle.

Make sure all chemicals such as fertilizers, weed killers, insecticides or cleaning agents are stored out of reach on a high shelf or in a locked cupboard. They are harmful if digested and may also cause harm if they get on your bunnies fur.

If you water your plants from the base, make sure the watering trays can't be reached as it can be contaminated with plant food which could be harmful to your bunny if they try and drink it.

### Did you know
### What is the name of a baby rabbit call?

A baby rabbit is called a Kitten or Kit for short. They can also be called a Leveret, Bunny or Nestling. The term Bun comes from old English dialect, first recorded in the sixteenth century.

### Bunny proof checklist
- [x] Provide a fully bunny proofed pen for your bunny to spend time in when they are unsupervised.
- [x] Next you need to make sure all the electrical cables are inaccessible to your bunny when you let them out.
- [x] Bunnies love to chew carpet, cover problem areas with a mat to protect them.
- [x] Make sure your bunny cannot get under your couch and crawl inside.
- [x] Make sure your plants are bunny safe and watch for falling leaves.
- [x] Make sure your backyard is escape proof and any positions plans are fenced off.

## Step by step guide to litter training your bunny

If your bunny is new to litter training, then it is best that they learn through a series of gradual steps.

Special care also needs to be given to juvenile bunnies as they will need to learn how to use a litter tray as they develop. Follow this guide and you will see how litter training can be achieved without too much fuss.

Placing food over this area such as a hay rack or hanging treat as this will encourage them to stay there longer

### What you need to do first

**Senior Luna**
Egg basket from Tractor Supply. I hang it over the litter box. One of my foster babies thought it was a toy LOL

**Producer's Pride Egg Basket, 8 in.**
SKU: 100851899

**$6.99**
★★★★☆ 3.6 (22) Write a review ‹

The first step is to prepare a pen or other enclosure as a litter training area where the litter training can begin. Its going to be messy so cover the entire area with something to protect the floor underneath.

Then lay down something that is absorbent and can be cleaned out easily such as newspaper or wood shavings or hay.

Litter training is going to need to be on your bunnies terms and time scale so it's going to need to be big enough for them to binky in as they may be spending some time there.

Next you need to let your bunny establish a place they choose as a toilet spot inside their pen or enclosure. This will typically be in a corner next to a wall where they feel safe.

Once you recognize this place the trick is to encourage them to return to the same spot till you can eventually place a litter tray there.

Placing food over this area such as a hay rack or hanging treat as this will encourage them to stay there longer. It is common to let bunnies eat hay over their litter tray throughout their lives to maintain good habits.

Bunnies go to the toilet regularly so if you do let your bunny out to roam freely away from a litter training area make sure to put them back frequently for small periods at a time so they can re-orientate themselves.

If you let them out for too long it is likely they will try and establish another corner in the room as a toilet.

It's important to keep all other areas very tidy and odor free by cleaning up any mass thoroughly.

You will get the odd accident so it's important that any smell left behind are removed as this will encourage them to go to the toilet there again.

If it can be washed, then put it in the wash, if it's a fabric surface you could use an odor control spray.

When you clean their corner out, hold back some of the mess and mix it back in each time so it retains a familiar smell and they can find it easily.

You can then start to put down some of the litter you want to use in this corner as it will help this spot establish itself as different to the rest of their enclosure.

At the end of this stage your bunny should be happy using a single spot and returning there when they need the toilet.

Remember to remain patient and progress at their speed because if you move too quickly you may break the habit and this process will take more time in the long run if you have to repeat yourself.

Let this continue for even a couple of weeks and hopefully you will notice your bunny will get tidier and tidier with its habits, then when you think the time is right take some of the litter and toilet waste, transfer this to a litter tray and place this over the spot and hopefully you bunny will take to it.

It is best to transfer some toilet waste every time you clean the litter tray out till you are confident it has been adopted.

You will know if it's too soon as your bunny is likely to go next to the litter tray or to another corner.

If you bunny is really not getting the hang of transferring to a new litter tray a trick that can be used is to lay a cotton bed sheet over the floor where they are pooping.

The idea is that because it removes any smells around the litter tray that your bunny may associate with a toilet area that may have permeated into flooring your bunny will stick to its litter tray better.

It's also useful as if they do go on the sheet you can tell instantly and whip it out and give it a wash.

### What's the best litter to use for my bunny

- Recycled paper based litters are very absorbent and odorless. Plus its compostable.
- Wood pellets are preferred by some people that don't get on with paper based litter.
- Sawdust is not the most suitable letter and is not recommended for adult regular use.
- Do not use cat litter, soil or sand in your bunnies litter box.
- Hay is good for encouraging your bunny to use its litter tray and works well alongside a more absorbent paper based litter.

## Using discipline when litter training your bunny

It is important to recognize the difference between bunnies and other domestic animals. Traditional toilet training for cats and dogs does use discipline or a certain amount of rubbing their nose in it as a part of the learning process. This type of training is not suitable for bunnies and will not be something your bunny will understand. In fact, any aggregation whether trying to teach a lesson or not is more likely to make them your bunny timid and harder to litter train.

**Boo**
I do this with boxes too!

Never shout at, scare, or hit your bunny, no matter how frustrating litter training is this will not help.

If you catch them in the act using another area, say a firm No! then take them to their actual litter tray.

When your bunny is safely out the way you will then need to clean up and make sure you remove any scent where the accident happened or your bunny will want to keep going back to this spot and add to it.

A stronger deterrent can be to keep a water mister to hand and when you catch your bunny misbehaving, spray a mist of cold water over them. Never squirt or spray water directly at them.

### Also see

**49**  How to discipline your bunny

**51**  How to use a water mister to train and discipline your bunny

# How to move your bunnies litter tray to a new place

It can be tricky moving your bunnies litter tray from its regular spot to a new place in your home as this can disturb you bunnies litter training habits.

If your bunny can't easily find their way to their litter tray or doesn't like where it's been moved too they may continue to use the area where it was before or even try and establish a new toilet area of their own choosing.

If you are planning this follow these simple steps from people that have done this and discovered all the pitfalls to this delicate process.

It doesn't take much to upset your bunnies litter training habits, follow these steps and avoid the pitfalls

## Follow these steps

When you first move the litter tray make sure you do everything you can to encourage its use.

An easy way to do this is to move your bunnies food next to it. If you have a hay feeder, place this above the litter tray so your bunny spends more time there.

### Bugsy
After some trial and error I think I got a good set up. I made my own hay hopper to avoid messes

Leave some litter still in the tray when you clean it out so it retains a familiar smell and your bunny can find it easily again.

This will help stop them starting a new spot as they will favor the one already used.

If they do try and establish their own toilet area in a different place, always quickly clean up any mess and smells so a habit does not form around it. If it was on a carpet it is best to use an odor control spray.

If your bunny does not take to using the litter tray in the new place and instead repeatedly goes to a different spot in the room it may be easier to move the litter tray there if it's not inconvenient.

Bunnies can be very stubborn. If your bunny keeps going back to the original spot you may need to move the litter tray back there or keep both of them.

---

### Bunny proof checklist
- [x] Move your bunnies food with their litter tray to encourage its use.
- [x] Leave some litter still in the tray when you clean it out so it retains a familiar smell.
- [x] Clean up all traces of mess and smells from the old place using fabric spray.
- [x] Bunnies can be very strong willed. You may end up moving the litter tray back in the end or to a spot they choose.

# How to discipline your bunny

**Inside this article**

Using any sort of discipline with a bunny is going to be tricky as they often don't respond well to it. At best you will be able to offer them some gentle guidance away from one activity to something more suitable. At worst you could make them antisocial or even aggressive towards you.

Also timing is everything. It is most often the case that by the time you notice your bunny has been up to something naughty their attention has moved elsewhere. It is likely they will have forgotten what they were doing, so any telling off you give them is wasted and could make your bunny unfriendly towards you.

Bunnies have strong natural instincts which you may need to learn to live with

However, if you do catch your bunny in the act it is possible to offer calm but firm guidance as to what's acceptable behavior and what's not.

We hope the advice in this guide shows you how to do this as kindly as possible.

## How to use gentle discipling with your bunny

It's important to realize that bunnies have very strong wild instincts and are often only doing what's natural to them. Remember discipline is not punishment, the aim is to discourage bad behavior and possibly to stop it.

When you bring a bunny into your home you have to accept some compromises by removing temptations, by being patient when they do something inappropriate and forgiving and forgetting pretty much immediately so you can focus on activities that are acceptable and reinforce good behavior.

Fortunately, there are a few things you can do that can help stop unwanted behavior and still leave you being the best of friends.

Firstly, never push or hit or grab your bunny, discipline is not punishment and your bunny will simply not understand physical discipline.

Unlike dogs for instance where you may steer their behavior with a firm touch, any sort of physical aggression with a bunny can trigger antisocial behavior leaving them permanently upset.

This can make your bunny fearful of you, turning away from you and ultimately making them less affectionate as a result. It may even result in them becoming aggressive back towards you.

Shouting or loud clapping should also be avoided. Bunnies have very sensitive hearing and loud noises can also trigger a fear response that will ultimately lead to timid or anti-social behavior.

Only use discipline when you catch your bunny in the act or any telling off will be wasted.

If it's a second afterwards they won't associate the punishment with what they are doing, and it will be wasted.

The best way to let your rabbit know it's not allowed to do something is by saying their name followed by a firm NO!

If they keep going back to their naughty behavior then take them away from the situation and give them something more interesting to do and encourage them by spending time with them.

If this is having no effect, then you may want to try using some stronger methods of telling your bunny off. Why not try using a water mister, the cold mist will deter them without causing them harm.

### Also see

**51**  How to use a water mister to train and discipline your bunny

### What to do if your bunny is aggressive towards you

Bunnies usually show aggression because they are afraid or frustrated with something, usually food, or because they want to defend their territory like their litter tray. This behavior can include nipping, biting, boxing or jumping at you.

If your bunny has become aggressive towards you or is behaving antisocially you should try and gain their trust again before you use discipline to correct any behavior.

Approach your bunny quietly and calmly, being careful not to startle them.

Some bunnies don't seem to enjoy being handled so don't try and pick them up. Sit or crouch down beside them and let them come to you. Some treats can help to gain their trust.

Lastly its worth noting that changes in rabbit usual social behavior can sometimes be a sign that your bunny is feeling unwell or in pain. If you're concerned, speak to a vet specialising in exotic pets.

**Did you know**

**Does discipline work with bunnies**

Using discipline with a rabbit is very different to cats and dogs. Dogs grow up in social groups and kittens have the guidance of their mother. These natural instincts to learn behavior have been developed further through domestication which ultimately helps us live side by side.

Rabbits on the other hand are hidden by their mothers mostly undisturbed when they grow up so they learn to survive on their own.

They are still very much wild animals and don't have many boundaries either as they grow up or in adult life, so setting boundaries for them is very hard to achieve and can be misunderstood by them.

### Bunny proof checklist

- [X] Only use discipline when you catch your bunny in the act or any telling off will be wasted.
- [X] Never shout at, scare, or hit your bunny as this sort of overreaction can make them timid, antisocial or even aggressive towards you.
- [X] The best way to let your bunny know it's not allowed to do something is by saying their name followed by a firm NO!
- [X] A stronger deterrent can be to keep a water mister to hand and when you catch your bunny in the act, spray a mist of cold water over them.

# How to use a water mister to train and discipline your bunny

It can be very frustrating if your bunny develops a persistent problem like chewing your baseboards, carpet, wallpaper or furniture.

This is where some bunny parents have found a blast of water from a mister can help persuade your bunny to stop.

The idea being the cold mist will firstly stop your bunny doing whatever it was doing, then hopefully the association of this happening every time they start up again will make them choose something else to do instead.

**Ozric**
A water mister can help stop naughty behavior

## Take a look at this guide for the do's and don'ts of this discipline technique.

Learn how to set boundaries and use simple training and gentle discipline to stop your bunnies unwanted behavior.

Only ever use the mist setting NOT the water jet setting if it has one.

If you blast your bunny with a jet of water this could not only be harmful if you catch areas around the eyes, nose or ears, it could also be stressful and your rabbit could develop aggressive behavior towards you or become antisocial and timid.

Only use discipline when you catch your bunny in the act or any telling off will be wasted.

If it's a second afterwards they won't associate the punishment with what they are doing.

It can also be tricky to get close enough when they are in the act as they may be wary of you approaching with something in your hand so it is best to sneak up on them.

Do not soak your rabbit, if they don't move when you try this you may want to try something else.

As you are doing this say a firm No as they associate this word with punishment and then lead them towards something better to do.

You can pick up a water mister from most gardening shops very cheaply, if you are repurposing something make sure it does not have any chemical residue in it from a previous use.

**Kuro**
There's no bunny proofing against flip flops right?

# How to stop your bunny peeing on your bed

If you decide to let your bunny free roam on your bed, if you're lucky you will be able to leave your bunny and never have to worry. However some people find it's more common to return to discover their bunny has gone for a pee on their bed instead.

This problem can start anytime and when it starts it can become incredibly frustrating, spoiling the time you spend together with changing sheets.

If you feel like you have tried everything and the only option is to ban your bunny from the bed then try this guide. We hope to show you that in a few simple steps and with a bit of perseverance you can get your bunny to share this space.

**Onion**
I've bested him this time! No more peeing down the side of my bed for this little guy. Vinyl table protector and Velcro.

## Why you bunny pees on your bed and how to stop it

If your bunny has started peeing on your bed don't worry it's not uncommon and in the following guide we hope to show you why it can happen and how to try and correct this behaviour.

Firstly don't encourage the problem with your own behaviour. Avoid giving your bunny food, especially treats on your bed. It can be fun when they are mugging you for snacks however the more they feel they need to compete for food in an area the more likely it is they will want to mark this territory so it is important not to encourage this.

## Controlling your bunnies territorial behavior

Bunnies like most pets want to establish their place in our homes, they are territorial when it comes to competing for the things they want and one of the ways they will establish their place is by marking it with their scent.

This can just be a few chin rubs however they will often go a bit further and pee in an area to establish their place there. This can be especially true if you have not had your bunny spayed or neutered as they will have stronger instincts and drives around this behavior.

To start with, encourage your bunny to sit calmly in a space to the side of your bed that they can establish

If they are coming and going all night you may need to use a second litter tray closer to your bed as they can often try and start a new toilet area close to where they spend time.

Remember bunnies go to the toilet frequently so if you are supervising them when they are on the bed It's important for you to recognize when they will probably need to go to the loo and break away from what you are doing to literally lead them to their litter tray.

Some of the signs that your bunny is getting ready to go to the toilet is they will become fidgety, often grooming themselves, they may start to try and get to a corner position backing themselves into a corner.

as theirs then don't invade this space. If they become frigidity, kick them off for a bit, then let them try again calmly.

Remember it can take time for your bunny to establish their place on the bed so don't invade this space. If they become frigidity, kick them off for a bit, then let them try again calmly.

After a while they should feel comfortable enough to spend time in this space without marking it by peeing there.

Some bunny owners have said they have had success by letting their bunny have an old towel they are allowed to sit on that they don't clean, including if their bunny has peed on it. The idea is that your bunny loses its urge to keep marking it.

It is important to clean up any mess and make sure you remove any scent where the accident happened or your bunny will want to keep going back to this spot and add to it. If it's just some poops then toss these in the litter try and give the surface a quick spray with some fabric freshener.

If it's a pee stain then it's important to wash any covers that can be removed and soak out any moisture and again treat surfaces with a fabric freshener.

### Reasons why you bunny may be peeing on your bed

- You feed them treats on the bed. This excited state of mind can make bad behaviour worse.
- If you think they are trying to mark their territory, try laying an old towel out for them to get used to.
- If your bunny is a long way from their litter tray they may try and start a new one, you may need a second litter tray that's closer.
- Having your bunny neutered or spayed can help control their behaviour.

### Where the vets may help

In a lot of cases people find that having their bunnies spayed or neutered led to better litter training and toilet habits. Speak to an exotic vets and they will be able to advise you.

If your bunny has suddenly started peeing on your bed for the first time after many years of not doing this it's worth checking if this problem is being caused by restricted mobility which can come with age or a health problem.

If you think this is the case it is worth asking a Vet specializing in exotic pets who will be able to advise you. If it is the case, then you want to help your bunny to get on and off your bed to make getting to the litter tray easier.

### How to discipline your bunny for peeing on your bed

### Voice training

An unusual way to stop peeing accidents that works for some people is to use some voice commands. You can start this by noticing when your bunny on the litter tray then repeat a keyword to them like 'Wee Wee, Wee Wee'.n

If you catch your bunny peeing on your bed it can feel like a real disappointment having to spend time cleaning things up instead of spending time playing with your bunny.

However, it's also the best time to be cool headed and take steps to send a clear message to your bunny that this is bad behavior. In this simple guide we show you how to avoid this frustration and teach your bunny to share your home.

The first thing to recognize is you should only tell your bunny off if you catch them in the act. If you leave it till your bunny has jumped away then telling them off will be wasted as they will not remember what they have done and why you are chastising them.

If you do catch you peeing or pooping on your bed, it's important not to overreact. Never shout loudly or clap aggressively at your bunny, they have sensitive hearing, and this could cause them a lot of stress.

Never hit or forcefully remove your bunny, unlike cats and dogs they simply will not understand this type of discipline and its unlikely to deter them, physical punishment could even cause harm if they bolt and fall. Over time it can make them timid or even aggressive towards you.

Instead say their name and NO! in a firm voice, even repeating this a few times. If your bunny is used to being picked up, then scoop them up or if not usher them into their pen or an area where they cannot come back into the room.

If your bunny keeps repeating this behavior then a stronger way of breaking this bad habit is to keep a water mister to hand and when you catch your bunny up to know good, spray a mist of cold water over them.

### Also see

**51**  How to use a water mister to train and discipline your bunny

Then if you think your bunny needs the litter tray next time you lead them to it repeating the words again along the way. This will help your bunny understand what it is you are doing differently to other activities.

# How to stop your bunny peeing on your couch

**Inside this article**

When you share your home with a house bunny it can also mean sharing access to your couch. Most of the time this doesn't cause any problems till that one time when out of nowhere your bunny decides it's their new litter tray.

When this habit starts it can be hard to stop and can eventually become incredibly frustrating, spoiling the time you spend together.

In this guide we run through most of the common causes and solutions to this problem.

We have tips from bunny parents that have fixed this problem so you can learn how to get things back to normal.

**Onion**
Some times stronger measures are needed

We also talk about the best way to tell your bunny No! if you catch them and what if any health problems could be causing this.

## Why does my bunny pee on my couch and how do I stop it?

Peeing and pooping accidents are not an uncommon problem for people that share their couch with their bunnies. If this is the case, read to see what can lie behind this problem and the best way to remedy the situation before it becomes a habit.

### Don't encourage problems

Avoid giving your bunny food, especially treats on your couch. It can get them over excited and this competitiveness can result in them choosing to mark this territory by weeing on it. It is best to keep them in a calm state when they are on the couch with you.

Bunnies also tend to like to go to the toilet where they eat so you want to avoid any association between feeding and pooping and peeing.

### Judging when they need to go

If your bunny is very comfortable or is being given a consent supply of cuddles or treats on your couch, they may decide that rather than going to their litter tray they will simply go to the toilet where they are.

They go to the toilet frequently so It's important for you to recognize when they will probably need to do this and break away from what you are doing and literally lead them to their litter tray before it's too late.

Some of the signs that your bunny is getting ready to go to the toilet is they will become fidgety, often grooming themselves, they may start to try and get to a corner position backing themselves into the corner.

However, this may not always be the case and they will simply pee where they are sitting!

## Controlling your bunnies territorial behavior

Bunnies like most pets want to establish their place in our homes, they are territorial when it comes to competing for the things they want and one of the ways they will establish their place on the couch is by marking it with their scent.

This can just be a few chin rubs however they will often go a bit further and use this area as a toilet to really establish their place there. This can be especially true if you have not had your bunny spayed or neutered as they will have stronger instincts and drives around this behavior.

**Tom and Barbara**
Great example of teamwork.

If they do jump up on the couch with you on it don't let them get in between you or someone else.

Also avoid letting them jump about on you or on the back of the couch as this dominating behavior is likely to be a part of them trying to compete with you which could lead to them trying to mark a spot you are in.

Instead encourage them to sit calmly in a space to the side of your couch that they can establish as theirs then don't invade this space. If they become frigidity, kick them off for a bit, then let them try again calmly.

After a while they should feel comfortable enough to spend time in this space without marking it by peeing there.

Some bunny owners have said they have had success by letting their bunny have an old towel they are allowed to sit on that they don't clean, including if their bunny has peed on it. The idea is if you give your bunny its own spot it will lose its urge to keep marking it.

## Where the vets may help

In a lot of cases people find that having their bunnies spayed or neutered led to better litter training and toilet habits. Speak to an exotic vets and they will be able to advise you.

If your bunny has suddenly started peeing on your couch for the first time after many years of not doing this it's worth checking if this problem is being caused by restricted mobility which can come with age or a health problem.

If you think this is the case it is worth asking a Vet specializing in exotic pets who will be able to advise you.

If it is the case, then you want to help your bunny to get on and off your couch to make getting to the litter tray easier.

### Reasons why you bunny may be peeing on your bed

- If you feed your bunny treats on the couch they will get over excited which can amplify bad behaviour.
- Your bunny could be trying to mark their territory, try laying an old towel out for them to get used to.
- If your bunny is a long way from their litter tray they may just be lazy and be trying and start a new one.
- Having your bunny neutered or spayed can help control their behaviour.

## What to do if you catch your bunny peeing on your couch

If you catch your bunny peeing on your couch it can feel like a real disappointment having to spend time cleaning things up instead of spending time playing with your bunny.

However, it's also the best time to be cool headed and take steps to send a clear message to your bunny that this is bad behavior.

In this simple guide we show you how to avoid this frustration and teach your bunny to share your home.

The first thing to recognize is you should only tell your bunny off if you catch them in the act.

If you leave it till your bunny has jumped away then telling them off will be wasted as they will not remember what they have done and why you are chastising them.

If you do catch you peeing or pooping on your couch, it's important not to overreact. Never shout loudly or clap aggressively at your bunny, they have sensitive hearing, and this could cause them a lot of stress.

Never hit or forcefully remove your bunny, unlike cats and dogs they simply will not understand this type of discipline and it is unlikely to deter them, physical punishment could even cause harm if they bolt and fall. Over time it can make them timid or even aggressive towards you.

Follow this simple advice and help guide your bunny away from behavior that spoils yours time together

Instead say their name followed by a firm NO! even repeating this a few times. If your bunny is used to being picked up, then scoop them up or if not usher them into their pen or an area where they cannot come back into the room.

When your bunny is safely out the way you will then need to clean up and make sure you remove any scent where the accident happened or your bunny will want to keep going back to this spot and add to it.

If it's just some poops then toss these in the litter try and give the surface a quick spray with some fabric freshener.

If it's a pee stain then it's important to wash any covers that can be removed and soak out any moisture and again treat surfaces with a fabric freshener.

As a last resort you can give a stronger message by using a water mister filled with water. Then when you catch your bunny in the act you can spray a mist of cold water over them to put them off.

### Also see

**51**   How to use a water mister to train and discipline your bunny

Voice training

An additional way to stop peeing accidents that some people say does work for them is to teach their bunny voice commands.

You can start this by noticing when your bunny is going to the potty and repeat a keyword to them like 'Wee Wee, Wee Wee'.

Then when you think your bunny needs the litter tray next time you lead them to it, repeat the words over again along the way. This will help your bunny understand that this is a special activity.

Given enough time and practice the idea is you will be able to use this voice command when you think your bunny needs the toilet and you will find they will often trot off on their own and come back when they are done.

---

### Bunny proof checklist
- [x] Avoid giving your bunny food, especially treats on your couch. This can complicate their behaviour.
- [x] Let your bunny adopt an old blanket you keep unwashed to stop them marking new territory.
- [x] Only tell your bunny off if you catch them in the act as they have very short memories and may become unfriendly.
- [x] Always clean up all traces of mess or it could be habit forming.

# How to stop your bunny peeing on your carpet

### Inside this article

If you have litter trained your bunny it can be very disappointing if they suddenly without any reason start peeing on your carpet.

This bad habit when it starts can also be hard to stop and you can end up spending the time you should be enjoying together worrying about it happening again or tidying up the mess.

In this guide we show you how other bunny moms have fixed this problem. We have suggestions as to what may be triggering this behavior and show you what you can do to break this habit so things can go back to normal.

We also talk about the best way to tell your bunny No! if you catch them and what if any health problems could be causing this.

It is very disappointing when your bunny suddenly starts peeing on your carpet. This bad habit when it starts can also be hard to stop

## Re-litter training a bunny that's peeing on your carpet

Putting some yummy hay over your bunnies litter tray can encourage them to use it more

If your bunny starts peeing on your carpet the first thing to do is go back to some basic litter training principles.

Make sure your bunnies food and water bowl or feeder are right next to their litter tray and avoid giving your bunny food, especially treats away from this area.

Bunnies are quite happy going to the toilet where they eat so by bringing these things together you can build up good litter training habits again. It's good to even put their hay feeder right above their litter tray.

If you have moved home, moved the litter tray from its regular spot or introduced your bunny to an additional space in your home, this can cause confusion and break their litter training.

Sometimes just moving furniture around in a room can all disturb your bunnies litter training routine and if they can't easily find their usual spot they may try and establish a new area to go in, typically on your carpet in the corner somewhere. If you think this is the case, you may need to go back to basics and re-litter train your bunny.

Bunnies like most pets want to establish their place in our homes, they are territorial and one of the ways they will establish their place in a room, especially if it's a long way from their litter tray, is by marking it with their scent.

This can just be a few chin rubs however they will often go a bit further and try and start a new toilet spot. You may need to accept you will have to put a second litter tray in the area they have favored. Not ideal for everyone but it can stop the mess.

Another reason your bunny may have an accident can be due to their reluctance to go to their litter tray because they are content where they are.

If for instance you are giving your bunny lots of cuddles or treats on the carpet, they may decide they would rather stay there then go to their litter tray so will simply go to the toilet where they are.

## Where the vet may help

In a lot of cases people find that having their bunnies spayed or neutered can reduce unwanted toilet behavior. Speak to an exotic vets and they will be able to advise you.

If your bunny has suddenly started peeing on your carpet after many years of good litter tray habits then it's worth checking if this problem is being caused by restricted mobility which can come with age or a health problem.

If you have noticed an older bunny slowing down or a change in your bunnies general behavior speak to a Vet specializing in exotic pets that will be able to advise you.

If this is the case, make sure your bunny has easy access to their litter tray without having to climb over high sides or obstacles to get there.

## What to do if you catch your bunny peeing on your carpet, training and discipline.

If your bunny seems to have forgotten its litter training and suddenly starts peeing on your carpet this can be really upsetting and unfortunately even though it's easy to do, telling them off for doing this will probably not stop them.

However, some gentle and well-judged guidance will help and in this guide we give you some simple rules to discipline your bunny without causing harm or causing antisocial behavior.

Only use discipline when you catch your bunny in the act or any telling off will be wasted. If it's a second

They go to the toilet frequently so It's important for you to recognize when they will probably need to do this and break away from what you are doing with them and literally lead them to their litter tray before it's too late.

Some of the signs that your bunny is getting ready to go to the toilet is they will become fidgety, often grooming themselves, they may start to try to back into a corner of where they are.

That said this may not always be the case and they will simply pee where they are sitting mid cuddle!

afterwards they won't associate the punishment with what they are doing, and it will be wasted.

Never shout at, scare or hit your bunny as this sort of overreaction won't discourage them and in the long run can make them timid, antisocial or even aggressive towards you.

The best way to let your bunny know it's not allowed to do something is by saying their name followed by a firm NO! Then take them somewhere you can leave them while you tidy up the mess.

When your bunny is safely out the way you will then need to clean up and make sure you remove any scent where the accident happened or your bunny will want to keep going back to this spot and add to it.

If it's just some poops then toss these in the litter try and give the surface a quick spray with some fabric freshener.

If it's a pee stain then it's important to soak out any mess and again treat surfaces with a fabric freshener.

A stronger deterrent can be to keep a water mister to hand and when you catch your bunny being naughty, spray a mist of cold water over them. Never squirt or spray water directly at them.

## Also see

**49**   How to discipline your bunny

**51**   How to use a water mister to train and discipline your bunny

# Traveling in a car with your bunny

Sometimes you may need to travel in your car with your bunny for more than the short trip to the vets that they are used to.

Bunnies are OK with longer trips however you will need to plan a few extra things to make sure they are comfortable and have everything they need. In this guide we show you what you will need to do to make the trip successfully.

**Bear**
Bear strapped in and ready to go to the vets

## Gathering the things you will need

First make sure you have a suitable carry case, it needs to be big enough to allow your bunny to move around in to get comfortable but not overly large or your bunny could be thrown around.

A small dog carrier can be ideal for this as they are typically a bit bigger than a normal bunny carrier and have a bigger hatch which makes it easier to attend to your bunny.

A front facing carrier can help you keep an eye on your bunny.

Carriers with a front facing entrance are available and these are ideal if you are traveling with your bunny on the back seat so you can keep an eye on them.

It is best to put something absorbent on the bottom of the carrier like a towel, hay, or newspaper.

This will help stop your bunny sliding about and absorb any toilet mess. If it's a long journey you may want to bring some spare bedding along so you can swap them if it gets soiled.

A good alternative to a regular carrier is to invest in one specifically designed for transporting dogs that has an elevated floor panel so any pee will drain away.

Next make sure your bunny has access to water. You can get water feeders you can attach securely to the front of the cage if your bunny is used to using a bottle.

You may find your bunny is too stressed out to use this so if it's on a long journey it is worth stopping occasionally and offering the water feeder directly with some encouragement by giving it a squeezer or by putting some water in a bowl.

It's best not to try and leave a bowl of water in the crate when you are moving as it is likely to spill or get knocked over, again plan a few regular stops where you can offer your bunny some water in its bowl.

If your bunny is used to eating wet food, it can be good to feed it some greens or a bit of fruit before you go and on the trip to help with hydration.

Bunnies need to eat regularly so make sure they have a good feed before you go.

Your bunny may refuse food and water when traveling which is normal if they are in unfamiliar surroundings so if it's a long journey make sure you plan a few stops where you give your bunny time to relay and eat if they choose to.

**Bear**
We love our front facing carriers for longer journeys so you can keep an eye on Bear. He likes to keep an eye on us too

You will need some way to secure your bunny in the car as it can be dangerous just leaving it on a seat in case you break sharply and it moves about.

To do this, put the carrier on the seat, you may need to wedge something underneath to make it level, then stretch the seat belt over the carrier so the belt wraps around the front of the carry case.

It's not ideal putting the carrier in the boot as it is going to be noisy in there and it can be hard to judge the temperature which can reach extremes of hot or cold. If it's a large crate you can obtain a seat belt extension that will make things easier.

Make sure your bunny is the last thing you put in the car before you leave and the first thing you take out when you arrive.

If you are traveling with a passenger, place the crate on the back seat across from them so they can keep an eye on it easily.

To make the trip more comfortable for your bunny make sure the temperature inside the car is moderate and never leave your bunny in the car when you are not there as the temperature can change inside rapidly.

Remember bunnies lose heat through their ears so if it starts getting hot open the window to let a breeze in or turn the inside fans on.

If it's sunny then you can help provide shade with some window shade screens.

## What you will need when you travel in a car with your bunny

- A carrier that can be secured with a seat belt
- An absorbent mat or a hay bedding to keep your bunny dry
- Some way of offering water along the way or at stops
- Some treats in case your bunny is hungry

Pack yourself first then pack your bunny stuff away to minimize the amount of tie your bunny is in its carrier.

If your bunny is used to you talking to them and making a fuss, then give them lots of words of reassurance during the journey.

It is best to keep the radio down low as excessive noise may cause additional stress.

## Bunny proof checklist

- [x] The carrier needs to be big enough to allow your bunny to move around in.
- [x] Strap the carrier in using the seat belt,
- [x] Make sure you stop regularly to see if your bunny wants a drink or any food.
- [x] Don't make too much noise in the car.
- [x] Plan ahead how you are going to bring your bunny in.

# How to build a bunny enclosure

### Inside this article

It's important to have an enclosure in your home where you can keep your bunny safely when you are at work or at night or when they are unsupervised.

Although you can buy bunny cages in pet stores, many people find their bunnies outgrow these spaces and then choose to expand them into an enclosed area. This gives their bunnies space to binky about and leaves enough room for toys and other essentials like litter trays and hay feeders.

In this guide we show you how to build a typical indoor enclosure, commonly used by many bunny owners and where the best place is to put it in your home.

How to set up a secure enclosure to put your bunny in when at work or at night

We also have a guide to how big it should be and ideas for the best flooring to use.

## What you need to build a bunny enclosure

The simplest way to build an enclosure is to use one or more pet pens to create a perimeter fence.

These come in a pack of large sheets of wire fencing that can be clipped together, look out for ones with a gate built into them which can give you access without having to un-clip or climb over the fence to get in.

These fences come with plastic clips or systems where they slot together or are secured using cable ties.

Remember bunnies, especially young kits can be good climbers so make sure it's a full-sized fence, the bigger the better.

You may want to keep an eye on it at first to see if your bunny can climb out. If so, you will need to either build the sides up a bit or put a cover over the top.

Some pens come with covers which can be great if your bunny is a bit of an escape artist.

It can be helpful to build the enclosure around a more secure cage such as a bunny cage or large dog cage. This can be a place of security and shelter inside the enclosure for your bunny and help you manage the space.

This can all be clipped together using cable ties which will make the whole structure more solid.

### What's the best type of bunny enclosure

- A very common enclosure is made of a pet pen lashed to a large wire dog cage.
- If you can afford the space a utility room or spare bedroom can be converted into a bun room.
- Multi level condos can be build out of wire grids and cable ties
- Even large purpose built cages and hutches can be a bit small for a bunny.

## How big should I make my bunny enclosure

There is no limit to the maximum space you can give your bunny and the bigger the better so this really comes down to how much space you can give up in your home. You do need to be careful about the minimum space required and you can find some good advice regarding this on the RWAF website.

### Winters luxury pen
Bunnies need lots of room to stretch out and relax

You should consider the minimum space to be big enough for your bunny to carry out its natural behaviors such as hopping about, at least three steps, it needs to be able to stretch up and reach its full height.

You will also need extra room for the other things inside such as a litter tray, water bowl or feeder, hay feeder and some toys and a hideaway. Remember bunnies can pick up quite a lot of speed when they binky about so you don't want them crashing into things.

## Where is the best place to put my bunny enclosure?

You will need to find somewhere calm for your enclosure to live, remember bunnies don't like loud noises and are easily scared so avoid chaotic spaces like a utility area with noisy appliances or kitchen or pantry where there are food smells that may be disturbing.

Rooms where children play can also disturb your bunny and if they are in a den make sure it is not next to stereo speakers or a TVs to avoid loud amplified noises.

Lastly make sure the temperature in the room is even and does not overheat in the summer or get too cold in the winter and conservatories that get very hot can be unsuitable.

Check for drafts at floor level as this can be uncomfortable for your bunny.

The best place is a heated and ventilated room in your home that does not get much traffic and is not in direct sunlight so your bunny can be safely left alone to relax.

## What the best floor to use in my bunny enclosure

Bunny enclosures can get a bit messy so it's best to cover the floor to stop any damage occurring.

This can also offer a bit of insulation and add a bit of grip to slippery floors to stop your bunny sliding about.

It can be especially helpful to cover carpeted floors which can be hard to clean and get damaged from by your bunny chewing them.

### Stan and Marv
With a bit of bunny proofing a utility room can make a great bunny space

**Typical floor covering used for house bunnies**

- Carpet off-cut, you can pick these up at a discount piece in most carpet stores.
- Children's play mats as these are tough and easy to wipe clean, keep an eye on these to see if it's being eaten as this may be harmful.
- Rugs or blankets, make sure it is made of a natural material, avoid synthetic materials with a rubberized back or strands of synthetic material in case your bunny chews them.
- Horse mats are super tough and can be cut to size.

### Also see

**65**    What is the best floor for my bunny enclosure?

# What should I put in my bunny enclosure?

**Inside this article**

When you pop your bunny in its pen at night or when you are at work your bunny is going to need a few things inside it's enclosure to keep them healthy and happy.

In this guide we take a look at the essential things you will need in your enclosure or pen and so you can be sure you have not missed anything important.

We also have some ideas on what other bunny parents used to enrich these environments to stop their bunny gets bored and make them feel comfortable.

Don't overload your bunnies enclosure as they need lots of space to hop about.

## The essentials you should have in your bunny enclosure

One of the first things to think about is the best location for the litter tray. It is best to situate this in a corner as bunnies prefer to use their toilet somewhere less exposed but it also needs to be easily reached to make cleaning it out less of a chore.

Make the litter try more fun by putting a hay rack above it

If your rabbit is new to its enclosure or learning litter training, then you may need a large tray till it gets used to it. Later on, you may be better off with a smaller corner litter tray as these will give your bunny more floor space.

Corner trays can also be helpful as they have a high side which can stop some of the mess spreading away from the enclosure.

Once you or your bunny has picked the best spot for the litter tray it is best to put your bunnies food right next to it as this will encourage good litter training habits.

**Charlie and Chester**
So these 2 rascals nearly gave me a heart attack tonight. I attach their hay feeder to the pen as they just drag it everywhere if I don't. Every now and then they shake it and the bit of wire comes loose. I usually find it easily but today it got swept up with old hay. Just spend the past hour checking through the old bagged hay, litter and poop to find it. Was so worried they had eaten there litter tray cable tie

Most importantly you should provide easy access to lots of hay, this is often best delivered in a hay feeder situated above the litter tray as bunnies will naturally poop and eat in the same place so this encourages good litter training habits.

It's also a useful way of catching some of the loose hay that falls from the feeder to stop it spreading around. A food bowl should also be placed next to the litter tray that can be used to help contain food such as fruit or vegetables or pellet foods.

Your rabbit is also going to need access to water and there are two main options. You can use a bowl or a water feeder. Bowls are widely regarded as the best as they are more natural for bunnies to use however it can be a matter of preference as some bunny moms prefer feeders to avoid poop and other things contaminating the water. Again, it's best to situate this near the food station and litter tray.

### Enrichment ideas for your bunny enclosure

A typical bunny enclosure made from a cage and then extended with a pet pen.

You are also going to need to provide your bunny with lots of stuff to do while you are away, and each toy is useful in their own way. Remember you bunny is also going to need room to move about so don't fill all the space and It's also best to keep a store of toys aside so you can rotate them to keep them interested when the novelty wears off. Each rabbit has its own favorite toys and behaviors so as you learn these you will know what gets ignored and what to get more of.

Chew toys are great for stopping bunnies getting bored. They need a constant supply of fiber to help their digestion and wear down their teeth so having a few things they can munch on will help with this. Twiggy or grassy balls seem to be the favorite as well as grassy mats.

Toss toys are also a favorite toy for bunnies. In their natural habitat they would spend a lot of time arranging their warrens and customizing their surroundings so having a few things they can arrange, and chuck about will help satisfy this natural urge.

If you have enough space why not build a bunny room

To help provide a stimulating environment you can add a few platforms for your bunny to jump on or a ramp they can run up and down. You can get bunny castles or ramps in stores or if you have some DIY skills it can be easy to make them yourself.

Some rabbits like to have a bit of shelter that will make them feel more secure and give them a place to rest where they feel safe. There are lots of things you can use for this including pet tents, tubes or hideaways that will help satisfy this need. You don't always need to spend money either as a cardboard box will make a great hideaway and provide hours of fun for your rabbit to chew and customize into a den.

### What types of toys should I put in my bunny pen

- A cardboard box or wooden shelter
- Wooden toss or chew toys
- Willow balls or tunnels
- Grassy balls or hideaways
- A cardboard or cloth tunnel
- A digging box

Simple enclosures can work well if you bunnies spend lots of time playing out

# What is the best floor for my bunny enclosure?

Choosing the right floor surface of your bunny, especially in their pen or enclosure is very important.

It needs to stop the damage to carpet or wooden floors underneath from chewing and stains which can be costly to repair. It also needs to make cleaning easy especially around the litter tray.

Hard surfaces are not always the solution as some bunnies find it difficult to move and binky about without slipping and a floor covering here can make play more comfortable.

Throw a few rugs on the floor to add some protection.

It is also important in some cases to offer insulation from cold hard surfaces. Picking the right floor for your bunny can be tricky as there are a number of options bunny people choose from.

In this guide we look at some of the popular choices and give you the pros and cons so you can decide on the best option for you.

## Vinyl flooring

Vinyl flooring is a cheap way to cover a large area.

Vinyl flooring is a cheap option for covering a larger area. It can be easily cut to size and is wipe clean and stain resistant.

You will need to watch this in case your bunny starts eating it. If this is the case its best to swap this out with a more natural material.

DIY stores offer cheap outdoor carpet that can be very hard wearing, and they will cut these to size which means you can get something that fits without having to cut it down yourself.

## Rugs and mats

A simple option can be to buy a mat or rug to lay on the floor. They are hard wearing and best of all can be washed if they get stained.

If you rabbit likes to chew things then try and find a mat that's made from a natural material, avoiding mats with rubberized backing or long strands of synthetic fiber as these can cause problems if your bunny eats them.

**Roger**
We get a cheap outdoor rug that can't be torn up

## Carpet roll ends

A cheap option to cover a larger space can be to use carpet roll ends. Most carpet stores will have some cheap bits of unused carpet from a job that you can pick up at a discount price.

Try and find one that's pure wool if you can so you know it will be safe if your bunny eats it and avoid carpet with heavy foam backing.

Make sure it does not have big loops or heavy rubber backing

## Puzzle tiles and play mats

Another popular solution to cover an area of floor is to buy some children's puzzle mats.

These jigsaw like foam sheets are tough and easy to wipe clean, again keep an eye on them to see if it's being eaten.

Children's play mats are easy to keep clean

If you want a single floor covering that would be easy to clean, then some people have found that children's play mats are ideal. These colorful floor covers are tough and stain resistant.

## Horse stall mats

Some people swear by horse stall mats. They're thick enough that they won't bunch up, fairly inexpensive and easy to clean. You can also get them custom cut at a supplier.

**Bugsy**
Horse stall mats are good because they are thick enough that they won't bunch up.

## Grassy mats

If you want to cover a smaller area for instance inside an enclosure with something your rabbit will really like then you can use a pack of grassy mats, the type found in pet stores.

These are relatively cheap so you can buy a few of them at a time and your bunny will love sitting on them and eating them.

The only downside to these is that they can get a bit messy when they start to fall apart.

Grassy mats can be a tasty way to cover a small area.

---

**Bunny proof checklist**
- [x] Rugs and throws are easy to throw down and washable
- [x] Horse mats are very durable and can be cut to size
- [x] Carpet roll ends can be a cheap and easy solution to cover a large area
- [x] Puzzle mats and children's play mats are wipe clean area will protect the floor underneath
- [x] Grassy mats can be used to cover a small area

# Cider and Ruby's bunny enclosure with a real wooden fence

Having grown tired of the square grid look, Cider and Ruby got upgraded to this luxury pad with a clothesline to clip herbs on and a latched gate for easy access.

Cider (male) and Ruby (female), are 2-year old Holland lops who reside in New Jersey, USA. They are both fixed, and are good-natured rabbits fairly mellow, except when it's mealtime! They go nuts over their greens/veggies (breakfast and dinner) and also any pellet snacks or treats.

Check out Cider and Ruby luxury enclosure.

## Who lives in this amazing space?

Cider is our noisy boy, who is interested in anything that is going on in the room, whether we are just sweeping up, or the vacuum is running, or the girls are playing (we have 3 human kids as well). He is also a pro flopper and takes some serious naps.

Ruby is our messy girl, who has crazy fuzzy fur, and forgets her toilet training regularly, but she is as sweet as can be and tolerates her extra grooming quite well.

## How the enclosure was built

They don't destroy the baseboards, or walls, or furniture in the room. They do however, like chewing on the untreated pine that their hay rack, resting crate, and enclosure, are made from. The entire pen is created out of untreated pine slats and assembled with a nail gun and screwed into the walls.

It has a latched gate that allows us easy access for cleaning, and also allows us to enclose the rabbits at night or when the whole family is in their space for holiday gatherings (these are the only times they are locked-in. Because they are free roam all day, they don't try to escape too much, although they have both done it.

The flooring is tile, which they love in the summer months to keep cool, even though the room has air conditioning. As the weather turns cooler, we add mats and rugs to put a barrier between them and the cold floor.

The room does not have heat (it is an enclosed sunroom), so we are looking to add a heating element to keep the chill off in the dead of winter which members of the Bunnyproofing group were very helpful with their suggestions! We already have a heating pad from our passed outdoor cat, so we'll start with that.

Cider and Ruby, Holland lops

## What's in the enclosure

The enclosure includes their hay rack, water bottles, and litter pan. It also has a crate for resting in and for perching on top. There is also another soft hidey house/bed.

Cider's favorite thing is the clothesline that contains clips where we dangle extra herbs or treats from time to time. We really love the space, so we're hoping not to relocate them during the winter months, as we did last year. We only built the enclosure this past spring after tiring of the look of the square grid wall-look.

## Gracie Henry and Lolas bunny room

Take a look inside this amazing bunny pen that's not only big enough for three rabbis but has room for guests humans as well.

The wall to wall flooring is vinyl so it protects the floor below and can be moped. It has a large thin rubber based mat in the center which is light enough to go in a washing machine.

The dig box is half a kids swimming pool and also contains a fresh supply of cardboard boxes from a local shop which Henry chews into shape!

This amazing bunny is not only big enough for three rabbis but has room for guests humans as well

### Meet the bunnies

Meet Gracie Henry and Lolas

The bunnies share all the facilities in their enclosure

Henry is the white mini lop, Gracie is the butterfly mini lop, and the black rabbit is Lola, a rescue and the cuddle monster of the group.

The little hutch is Henry's den, they are never locked in it, it's just for fun.

They have this safe space to keep them safe but also have the run of the house and are in the garden free roam with French doors open to the house a couple of evenings a week.

Vinyl was laid over the floor to protects it and make it easy to mop out

Henry is obsessed with cardboard box dens. Gracie sleeps on the chair and Lola loves the dig box. Something for everyone.

Lola relaxing after a hard days playing

# How to build a digging box for your bunny

**Inside this article**

A digging box is one of the best free toys you can make for your bunny. All you need to do is fill a cardboard box with things your bunny would like to forage around in and they will be happy for hours, and the best thing is it contains all the mess.

In this guide we look at the pro's and Con's of different types of boxes and show you the best way to prepare a cardboard box.

We also go into details about what's good and bad to use as fillings for the box.

A bored bunny is a nighty bunny so keep them out of trouble by building one of these brilliant toys.

Build a digging box and let your bunny play without damaging your home or making a mess.

## How to build a digging box for your bunny

You can also try hiding some treats in there!

It's important for your bunnies happiness and health to enrich their environment and allow them to do many of the things they would naturally do in the wild. One such important activity is to forage for young roots and shoots in the undergrowth.

Unfortunately, this behavior in your home can turn into digging up your plant pots, tugging up your carpet or flooring or shredding your soft furnishings, cushions and shredding your wallpaper.

That's why digging boxes are such great toys that your bunny is going to want to play with over and over again. It satisfies your bunnies need to forage for food and also stops the mess from destruction going everywhere by containing it.

First choose a container big enough for your bunny to turn around in and low enough to easily jump in and out of.

Cardboard boxes are best as your bunny will enjoy chewing and wrecking them as well. Make sure you remove any tape or staples.

Next fill the box with anything you think your bunny will like. Straw, paper and old toilet roll tubes work well, Plastic and paper with heavy incs should be avoided. Sand and soil are OK but can be messy.

One additional benefit of a digging box is that it can be placed over a spot of carpet that is being chewed or up against an area of wallpaper that your bunny has been chewing or shredding. It's the perfect distraction to keep your bunny out of trouble.

Remember not all bunnies are diggers and yours might not choose to play in the box so don't be discouraged if it's not used straight away. You can encourage your bunny to play in it by placing the box somewhere you bunny will feel safe as if it's in the middle of the room your bunny may not feel comfortable burying its head in it. You can also try hiding some treats in there to make it more attractive.

Make sure you keep an eye on it and if your bunny starts eating a lot of the material or accidentally mistakes it for a litter tray and uses it as a toilet area, then it is best to get rid of it completely and maybe try again another time to break the habit.

## What to use for your bunnies digging box?

The first thing you are going to need is something big enough for your bunny and a load of stuff to fit in. Its purpose is also to contain the mess from the digging and shredding, so it needs to have sides high enough to keep the stuff inside but still allow your bunny to hop in and out.

Cardboard boxes make an excellent choice as they are free and can be changed from time to time if they become tatty and to keep interest. Make sure it's made of a safe material such as plain cardboard without heavy ink or a plastic finish and remove any tape or staples.

### Stan and Marv
So much noise coming from the rabbit room. I took the lid off this box to find the boys digging for freedom! This box was completely intact apart from the hole for the tunnel to enter it yesterday. Who needs posh toys?!

Plastic bowls or boxes will also work well although they can be slippery so make sure your bunny can get stuck inside. Some thin plastic storage containers can break leaving sharp edges so choose something robust.

A wicker basket would be great, you would expect it to get eaten though. Avoid anything that looks like it's been treated in heavy varnish in case it is chewed.

## What's the best filling to use in my bunnies digging box?

If you are thinking of making a digging box for your bunny or are looking for some new ideas as to what you can put in it to make it more interesting then we have put together this guide for you. We look at the good points and the bad points of some of the stuff people have tried in their digging box as well as things that should definitely be avoided.

If you are looking for some new ideas for things to put in your bunnies digging box then this guide for you.

The obvious thing to put in a digging box is soil or sand, however we would not recommend this as it can be very messy leaving dirt in your home that is kicked out or spread about on your bunnies feet. It also does not leave many options for putting things in there that your bunny can forage for.

The favorite choice of filler for most people is shredded paper, like waste from a paper shredder that's cut into strips like confetti. Paper based packing material also makes a great choice as it is typically unprocessed and often makes a nice scrunchy noise which is a bonus. If you put any paper in, avoid glossy print and make sure any staples are removed. It is best to avoid newspapers or magazines as the inks could be harmful if your bunny eats a lot of it.

### Ozric
Ozric loves his digging box especially when I hide some treats in the bottom of it

Straw and hay are also good digging box fillers as they are cheap and are also a good way of encouraging your bunny to eat more of them .

Don't use bubble wrap or the foam pellet or block fillers. Any synthetic material may be an issue as this can cause a problem if digested.

It's best not to put any sort of material you use in their litter tray as your bunny may easily confuse this new box with another so make sure you use something different. If your bunny does start using their digging box as a litter tray you will need to remove it in case you disturb their good litter training behavior.

### What are the best things to put in your bunnies digging box

- Shredded paper
- Toilet roll tubes
- Pinecones
- Straw
- Soil
- Sand

### Things you should NOT put in your bunnies digging box

- Glossy magazines
- Inky news paper
- Foam plastic packing material
- Litter

### Edison

Mid-day is his favorite nap time so we don't bother him then.

As well as a base material it can be good to throw in a few interesting things to give them something to forage for.

There are lots of chew toys you can buy from a pet store that will work well such as willow sticks and balls as well as wooden chew toys.

This can be a great place to give your bunny any of the chew treats you can buy as it will contain any mess as they fall apart.

### Raspberry

I read that bunnies loved to play and dig in ball pits, so I set up one for my bunny. She loved it and was chasing them all over my room and never caught the ball, which kept her busy for a while. However, she finally ended up catching one and looks like she ate a pretty big chunk out of it. I have been looking for the plastic piece around my room and can't find it, so I am worried she probably ate it.

You don't have to spend any money on toys for your bunnies digging box, toilet roll tubes, pine cones, and bunny safe twigs you can forage yourself can make the box just as much fun.

To keep your bunnies interested it is best to keep swapping the content out every so often so there are lots of new things to find. This will help remove any soiled materials and keep your bunny coming back to see what they can find.

### Bunny proof checklist

- [X] Take a large clean cardboard box and remove any tape or staples.
- [X] Fill the box with things your bunny would love like shredded paper, straw and old toilet roll tubes.
- [X] Check regularly to make sure it is not being used as a litter tray.
- [X] Avoid plastic packing and inky materials. Soil and sand can be messy.
- [X] Hide a few treats in the bottom to help keep your bunny interested.

# How to build your bunny a cardboard box hideaway toy

Most bunny owners discover that a simple cardboard box is one of the best toys you can give your bunny. Not only is it free, it will keep a bored bunny entertained endlessly as they customize it into their own special den.

It's also good in many other ways including giving your bunny something to chew on other than your baseboards and carpet, it will also help wear down your bunnies teeth which grow constantly through their lives and give them some extra dietary fiber which is essential to their health.

In this guide we show you how to prepare a box and what other bunny owners do with them to make them even more fun.

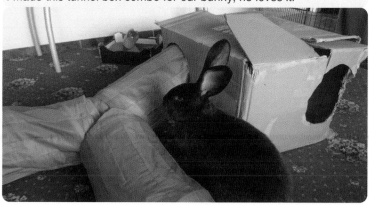

**Bear**
I made this tunnel box combo for our bunny, he loves it!

## How to make a cardboard box safe for your bunny

- Remove any staples or tape before you give it to your bunny
- Avoid boxes that have glossy surfaces or heavy print
- Avoid boxes that have stored toxic materials

## How to prepare the box

The first thing to do is choose the right box. It needs to be big enough for your rabbit to fit in comfortably so they can turn around. If it's a large box then make sure it is sturdy and can be folded up tightly so it does not collapse on your bunny.

Make sure it's made from plain cardboard without heavy ink printed on it or coloring and avoid boxes with plastic or shiny finishes, the more natural looking the better.

Also think about where the box may have been stored and what's been stored in it as this may have left chemical residues that could be harmful. The best sort of boxes come from supermarkets that once contained food as you know this will be the safest.

Next you need to prepare the box. It's important to remove any staples and tape as this can be dangerous if your rabbit eats it. Boxes that are glued together are also unsuitable. What you want is to be left with just the cardboard.

It is best to fold the flaps of the box over themselves so it holds together tightly. Place the box with the folded side on the floor. This can help stop your bunny falling through it if they jump on top of it.

**Bear**
What a brilliant idea from the people that sent me this box

It is best to cut a couple of holes in either side of the box to let your bunny pop in and out rather than leaving a side open as this will make the box stronger and last longer.

If you want to make this even more fun, you can try making a few boxes and setting them up as a mini warren or cutting a hole in the side and stuffing a tunnel into it.

Printed in Great Britain
by Amazon

84752256R00042